The Firefighter's Best Friend

Lives and Legends of Chicago Firehouse Dogs

Trevor J. Orsinger and Drew F. Orsinger

With Foreword by James T. Joyce, Commissioner,
Chicago Fire Department

First Edition

LAKE CLAREMONT PRESS

4650 North Rockwell Street • Chicago, Illinois 60625
www.lakeclaremont.com

The Firefighter's Best Friend
Lives and Legends of Chicago Firehouse Dogs
Trevor J. Orsinger and Drew F. Orsinger

Published September 2003 by:

4650 North Rockwell Street
Chicago, Illinois 60625
773/583-7800
lcp@lakeclaremont.com
www.lakeclaremont.com

Publisher's Cataloging-in-Publication
(Provided by Quality Books, Inc.)

Orsinger, Trevor J.
     The firefighter's best friend : lives and legends of
Chicago firehouse dogs / Trevor J. Orsinger and Drew F.
Orsinger. —1st ed.
          p. cm.
          Includes index.
          LCCN: 2003100218
          ISBN: 1-893121-20-8

     1. Fire departments—Illinois—Chicago—History.
     2. Working dogs—Illinois—Chicago—History.
     I. Orsinger, Drew F. II. Title.

     TH9505.C4O77 2003   636.7'0886
                    QBI03-200085

Printed in the United States of America by United Graphics,
an employee-owned company based in Mattoon, Illinois.

07 06 05 04 03   10 9 8 7 6 5 4 3 2 1

🔥 Table of Contents 🔥

⚱ **Foreword** ⚱

Firefighters love telling stories. Between alarms, meals, training, and shift changes, there are always stories—recalling, recounting, and reliving those moments of glory that always interrupt the firefighter's life. These stories are about the human spirit and belong to no one, so even when firefighters retire, their tales and memories live on in those who served with them. They are written into the very bricks of the firehouse.

What occurs every day, on every shift, in every house from the firehouses of the South Side to the fireboat resting on Lake Michigan is always the same: firemen and women telling their stories. Told from different perspectives, from the many firehouses of this great city, each time firefighters recall their tales, they preserve firehouse history. It's an "oral tradition," no doubt, and it's a legacy that is as priceless as those other virtues that firefighters value most: sacrifice, commitment, and bravery. If they didn't before, all Americans now realize how greatly firefighters prize these virtues. Their stories need to be remembered, written down, and preserved for America's next generation.

Trevor Orsinger and Drew Orsinger preserve that tradition for our city in *The Firefighter's Best Friend*, by recording the tales of that firefighter who is on duty 24 hours a day, 7 days a week, 365 days a year—the firehouse dog. The following pages

Lieutenant James Joyce with Dudley (1977).

capture the many stories of Chicago firefighters and their dogs. The Brothers Orsinger have listened for endless hours, spent many nights with various shifts, and were privy to a process that makes Chicago firefighting so unique. They have worked over different versions of the same stories and culled together definitive anecdotes in order to relive true moments of firehouse glory.

So enter the firehouse in these pages and share in the daily experience of those men and women who protect our neighborhoods every day. Sit at the kitchen table and laugh over the stories only dogs can inspire. The Orsingers have chosen those stories that will be told over and over again. From the comical to the heroic, this book makes sure that the oral tradition of the Chicago firefighter is kept alive and thriving. They trace a canine lineage from the Great Chicago Fire of 1871 to the dozens of "active" dogs in the city today. Chicago's history is deep, and it is no surprise that the city possesses one of the richest firedog traditions in the world. To my knowledge, no other city in the world has as many active firedogs in a single department as Chicago.

The relationship between fire department personnel and firedog is mutually beneficial. Many of the dogs are strays that find a home in the comfort of a Chicago firehouse. They are provided food and shelter in exchange for doing what they do best: being a dog. They are ardent protectors, dutifully guarding their house when the firefighters are away. Property is safeguarded and lives secured because of the extraordinary loyalty provided by today's firedogs.

The bond these canines develop with the men and

women they serve can be deeper than the connection between families and their pets. Nowhere is this more evident than in the dozens of plaques, gravesites, and memorials throughout the city that commemorate those firefighter dogs that have served Chicago so well. These dogs are members of their crews; they are companions and friends, and often become neighborhood playmates for those children in the city who do not have pets of their own.

In Carl Sandburg's famous poem, *Chicago*, he describes a city of "broad shoulders" and later declares that Chicago itself is as fierce as a dog. Perhaps he visited a Chicago firehouse before writing these lines. Chicago firefighters and firedogs share a fierce sense of loyalty and steadfast commitment to the citizens they serve. Chicago is a great city with unlimited traditions and history. But, as you read on, you will find that the tradition of the firedog may be among the richest.

— James T. Joyce,
Commissioner,
Chicago Fire Department

⛫ Preface ⛫

A tiny firehouse is tucked away in a little section of Chicago while snowflakes silently accumulate outside. Residential houses surround the station and though the firehouse's presence is seemingly out of place, it fits perfectly within the confines of the neighborhood. Residents have become accustomed to the sirens and bells. They understand that the regular bustling of the house is just a part of what makes the neighborhood so charming. Perhaps it is the fact that there is always a person inside the firehouse, or maybe it is because people know the firefighters are there to protect them, but the station exudes a certain majesty. It is a beacon of strength and safety for the community.

"Steamers," by Lee Kowalski.

When one thinks of a firehouse dog, an image of a red fire truck with lights flashing and sirens blazing frequently comes to mind. Within this vision, there is usually a black-spotted Dalmatian standing atop the hose-bed or nestled among rugged firefighters in the cab of the truck. Indeed, it is an easy picture for the mind's eye to grasp. This book memorializes a specialized facet of the often-unnoticed role dogs play in society—that of the dogs that have resided and worked in firehouses, specifically those in the city of Chicago.

We met our first Chicago firedog on New Year's Eve, 2000, at Engine 18, across the street from our high school alma mater, St. Ignatius College Prep. We were visiting our former pole-vault coach, firefighter John Pawelko. As we were talking, a large, veteran Rottweiler named *Sadie* emerged from the back of the house to greet us. John began telling us numerous stories about Sadie and by the time we left Engine 18, several other firefighters joined us to tell of her exploits. That night, we were privileged to taste a small piece of Chicago Fire Department history.

We immediately wondered how many other dogs lived in

Chicago firehouses and how many other stories existed. With such great material available, we naturally assumed someone had already incorporated these stories into a single work. Initially, a coffeetable version with high-gloss pictures and a few choice anecdotes seemed to be an appropriate form. To our surprise, the extent of published material on Chicago firedogs, or any firedogs, was limited. The only books written on the subject were primarily children's stories. Thus, we began the long journey of writing an in-depth review of Chicago firedogs throughout history.

Once we realized a serious book had never been written on the subject, we needed to find out how many firehouses had dogs. So we simply called every firehouse in the city. We learned there were 27 dogs, well actually, 25 dogs actively living in Chicago. *Lester* at Engine 50 was run over by a car a week before we called, and the other dog turned out to be a two-legged firefighter named Jake. We built a Web site, sent out flyers, followed every lead we received, and asked firefighters from all over the city to tell us their stories. Our research confirmed the existence of over 300 dogs that have lived in Chicago firehouses since the Great Chicago Fire of 1871. Because their presence was—and still is—rarely recorded, it is impossible to calculate just how many thousands of canines have served the city.

We will never know exactly how many dogs lived in Chicago's houses over the years, but every confirmed firehouse dog serving in the city of Chicago has been appropriately indexed for reference. Firefighters rarely stay in the same house for more than ten years, making it impossible to obtain a full firedog lineage for every house in the city. As a result, the quantity of our research is not as plentiful prior to 1950 because the pool of firefighters to interview has drastically declined. At times, the specifics were difficult to acquire, but it is in no way an indicator of fewer dogs living in the city. Usually, the most famous dogs are remembered vividly or recorded in some form. It is these accounts that we have sought to preserve.

While the typical account of a Chicago firedog is maintained within the firefighters' memories, there were a few main sources of written material on Chicago firedogs. In the 1950s, Hal Bruno wrote an extensive series of articles in the *Chicago American* newspaper featuring over 60 Chicago firedogs and any reference to a 1950s dog inevitably came from him. Reverend John McNalis and Ken Little, authors of both volumes of *A History of the Chicago Fire Houses*, provided us with a sound historical structure for the foundation of dates, times, and places. They also reminded us that there are no "fire stations" in Chicago, only firehouses. The Chicago Fire Museum at St. Gabriel's Church, and Batavia, Illinois, Mayor Jeff Schielke's collections provided us with invaluable records on firedogs. We also received meticulous documentation and pictures of *Felix* from Darlene Fillis, a retired librarian living in Palos Hills, Illinois. While these sources provided us with a substantial base for the book, the bulk of our material came from the firefighters themselves.

With so many stories and pictures, it is impossible to publish them all. Some houses have records of 20 dogs while others may have only one or none. For example, Engine 44 went through 12 different dogs in one year, and Engine 95 simultaneously cared for six dogs, three cats, and an opossum in the house's backyard.

What constitutes a Chicago firehouse dog? If a dog consistently spends (or spent) the night at a Chicago firehouse, we consider it an authentic Chicago firedog. Some firefighters bring their dogs to work during their shifts, and as long as the dog spends the night, it earns the right to be considered one of the crew. Each dog is categorized by the house in which it served. There may be two or three different houses that were home to the same engine or truck, so addresses tend to become more important with some of the older houses. Additionally, we have divided these stories into three sections: North, West, and South Side Firedogs. Our method for deciding where a house belonged within this framework was as follows: If the house is above or below Madison Street (Chicago's official dividing line between north and south) then it was labeled accordingly. If the house was further west than it was north or south, then it was labeled a West Side house. Otherwise, there is no particular order to these stories. Rather than placing them in a chronological fashion, we positioned them in a way that would be the most enjoyable for the reader.

Time tends to blur memories. Some fire department personnel have difficulty remembering when the dog lived at the firehouse even in contemporary times. We developed a flexible system designed to document the dog's existence in a historical perspective. The best measure of a dog's life is within the context of a "decade." We found it easier to use decades as a measuring stick for knowing when the dog served at a house.

There is something for everyone here. You will read about the heroic, the goofy, and the day-to-day behavior of these animals. You will learn of their service to the city as they climb ladders, sound the alarms, fight fires, save children, break up fights, roll hose, exterminate vermin, and protect property. But these dogs do more than just serve the Chicago Fire Department. Some of their varied hobbies include playing basketball, donating blood, "socializing" with other neighborhood dogs, starring in the news, and even riding the Chicago Transit Authority's (CTA) subway and bus systems.

Amazing births, tragic deaths, and unfortunate injuries are common. Some dogs pass away in the same house where they were born. Many firehouses have cemeteries or memorials devoted exclusively to the dogs that served there. Several dogs are buried beneath the same concrete of the house they patrolled. Injuries may occur from on-the-job activities or by being in the wrong place at the wrong time. You will learn about the three-legged dog named *Bear* as an example of the dangers these dogs face every day.

While approximately a quarter of the firedogs that have lived in the city of Chicago were Dalmatians, at least half were mutts. Close behind in popularity is the German Shepherd. Colorful names like *Lady of Flame* and *Schlitz* are mixed with the more common *Lady* or *Brown Dog*. The Dalmatian-influenced names *Dottie*, *Pepper*, and *Domino* are popular as well. There's also *Thirty,* named after the house and *Luverne*, named after the truck company that manufactures many of Chicago's fire engines. And, of course, no fire department would be complete without an *Ashes* or *Smokey*. The highlights are impossible to summarize, but the single most common element of all these canines is their connection to the Chicago firefighters. Without them, these dogs wouldn't be allowed to do what they do best.

No matter how the firehouse dog makes his or her entrance or how long they remain at the firehouse, they will have undoubtedly made an impact on the city and the fire department. As a result, the dogs that reside in these firehouses quickly leave a heritage that is filled with astounding stories and fond memories. Perhaps there is a reason why this book began in Chicago's oldest firehouse and across the street from one of the few buildings to remain after the Great Chicago Fire of 1871.

—*Trevor J. Orsinger*
and Drew F. Orsinger

The one absolutely unselfish friend that man can have in this selfish world, the one that never deserts him, the one that never proves ungrateful or treacherous, is his dog. A man's dog stands by him in prosperity and in poverty, in health and in sickness. He will sleep on the cold ground, where the wintry winds blow and the snow drives fiercely, if only he may be near his master's side. He will kiss the hand that has no food to offer, he will lick the wounds and sores that come in encounter with the roughness of the world. He guards the sleep of his pauper master as if he were a prince. When all other friends desert, he remains. When riches take wing and reputation falls to pieces, he is as content in his love as the sun in its journey through the heavens. If fortune drives the master forth an outcast into the cold, friendless and homeless, the faithful dog asks no higher privilege than that of accompanying him to guard him against danger, and to fight against his enemies. When the last scene of all comes, and death takes his master in its embrace and his body is laid away in the cold ground, no matter if all other friends pursue their way, there by his graveside will the noble dog be found, his head between his paws and his eyes sad, but open in alert watchfulness, faithful and true even to death.

—Senator George Vest of Missouri, 1870

Chapter 1

The Chicago Firedog in History

🚒 The Chicago Firedog in History 🚒

It's a slow January night, and there have been no fires. A faithful dog is lying down in a warm firehouse and perks his ears at the noise of laughter coming from the firemen playing cards. A hand reaches down to pet him and feed him a scrap of food leftover from dinner. There is genuine camaraderie among the men as they tell stories and recall times now forgotten. The dog remains at his post, constantly ready to join firefighters wherever they may go. This scene can be found in any firehouse around the world and at any time over the last 300 years.

The history of the firedog is intertwined with the oral traditions and isolated documents of fire departments

The men of Truck 21 and their Dalmatian (1910).

worldwide. The earliest notions of firedogs are linked to the most popular and traditional firedog: the Dalmatian. In order to understand why dogs came to have significant roles in firehouses, one must go back hundreds of years when Dalmatians ran alongside coach horses in Great Britain.

Contemporary firedogs are not always Dalmatians, but the breed maintains a well-founded association to fire departments. Although Dalmatians have been around for over 600

years, their entry into the world of firefighting began about 300 years ago. While there is some speculation that drawings of spotted dogs were memorialized in Ancient Egyptian ruins, the first confirmed image of the Dalmatian appeared on a wall painting in 1360 A.D. in Eastern Europe. The Dalmatian came from Dalmatia, a region off the coast of the Adriatic Sea, in what is now Croatia. But the English name "Dalmatian" was not used until the early 1700s when Great Britain began a formal breeding regiment for the canine.

The Dalmatian's use as a work dog started before their fire department characterization because of the dogs' ability to keep pace with horses. The breed is unusually strong for its size, able to run long distances without exhausting. This is why the English aristocrats were among the first known employers of the Dalmatian. The dogs often ran together in pairs, clearing the streets for the horse-drawn coaches and keeping other canines from scaring the horses. Eventually, the dogs became icons of social status—the more dogs surrounding the coach, the higher one's standing in society. In contemporary England, the Dalmatian is still referred to as a "coaching dog."

The fire departments in Great Britain were among the first to use the Dalmatians for the same reasons they were employed by the social elite. Before the invention of the automobile, firefighters hauled their equipment with horse-drawn wagons. Dalmatians cleared the streets for the oncoming pumpers, just as they cleared the streets for England's wealthy. When the fire alarm sounded, the Dalmatians were first out of the firehouse, barking in the streets to announce the approaching firemen's coach. Some firedogs continue this tradition by either proclaiming a rig's departure or by serving as an added "barking siren" when making a run to the scene of a fire.

Two distinct skills possessed by the Dalmatians made them an ideal complement to firehouses. The first was their ability to calm horses. Horses are known to be extremely afraid of fire. Despite this fear, horses were necessary to bring the fire coaches as close to the flames as possible. The presence of the Dalmatians was a needed distraction for the horses, allowing firemen to employ their equipment more effectively. As a result, Dalmatians played a vital role in firefighting procedures and were used extensively throughout Europe.

Dalmatians were also valued for their ability to protect horses from theft, a common occurrence before the industrialization of Europe. While the men were battling the fires, the dogs patiently guarded the equipment in the wagon. When the horses were not in use, the dogs meandered around the stables watching the possessions in the coach. Today, horses are no longer employed by the Chicago Fire Department, but almost every firedog continues to serve in this role as a protector of property and of the lives of the firefighters themselves.

The firehouse dog's ability to catch and kill rats has also been another valuable asset to a firehouse that continues in contemporary times. The Dalmatians enjoy hunting these critters while the firemen appreciate the extermination services they provide. Today, there are countless stories of firedogs killing rats in firehouses—some even expect a treat when they drop a dead rodent at the foot of a firefighter.

All of these attributes made the Dalmatian a natural fit for the firehouses of the 1700s. Many rumors circulate as to why Dalmatians are the mainstay of firehouse folklore. Among them is that the Dalmatian is deaf, and consequently less likely to become upset upon hearing the whistles, sirens, and flames that accompany life as a firedog. Some believe that the dog possesses extraordinary vision that allows it to see through smoke. Still others believe that the Dalmatian is attracted to the color red and therefore relishes time spent around fire engines. To our knowledge, none of these myths is true. Although some firefighters do claim that it *is* an established, biological fact that every time a Dalmatian goes on a run in Chicago, it grows a new spot on its coat.

Despite the legends associated with Dalmatians and other firedogs, the first canine officially documented by a fire department was *Chance* of the London Fire Brigade, in 1828. An unknown fireman who served in the London Fire Brigade for 50 years wrote to the editor of *The Fireman* magazine and stated that "fire after fire he attended until he was well known in London as 'Chance, the watermen firemen's dog.' Chance remained a faithful friend of the firemen for many years. He ultimately went nearly blind; even then he used to follow the engine."

Chance made quite an impact on the London Fire Brigade firefighters. While his breed was undetermined, Chance was known for following the crew to every fire and rescuing several people. He rotated throughout the firehouses in London, spending a few days at each house. As a result, every firefighter in London knew him. A collection was taken by firefighters to purchase a brass collar with an inscription that read, "Stop me not, but onward let me jog, for I am Chance, the London Firemen's dog." Chance also had his portrait painted by several artists. William Heath completed one of these paintings in 1834, depicting Chance against the background of a burning House of Parliament, pawing at a flowing hydrant while a fireman watched over him.

Upon his death, many London newspapers ran obituaries of the dog. One paper reported that while on his deathbed, Chance tried unsuccessfully to rise up and follow the men one last time as they rushed to a fire. When Chance passed away, his favorite house at the Central Station of the London Fire Brigade paid a taxidermist to stuff him and place him in a glass case. After the taxidermist completed his work, he decided to instead sell the famous dog to a showman on the other side of town, who let visitors glimpse the dog for a penny. The showman unknowingly allowed a fireman in for a viewing. Several hours later, the entire squad returned to retrieve their dog. The firefighters mounted the case on a wall in their firehouse with a plaque that read:

Chance, well known as the firemen's dog. Died October 10, 1835. This is humbly inscribed by the Committee of London Fire Establishment and their obedient servants.

The grandfather of the modern-day firedog, Chance proved to be the benchmark in a longstanding institution.

Though there is no known record of how the Dalmatian made its way across the Atlantic to America, it is believed that the founders of this country transported the dog with them when escaping the tyranny of King George III and forming the original 13 colonies. Though our country's first president, George Washington, is known for his love of Dalmatians, it is the statesman, philosopher, and inventor Benjamin Franklin who is credited with integrating the Dalmatian into the firehouses of America. As a former fireman himself, Franklin understood the necessity of canines in a large fire department. He encouraged the growth of the firehouse dog in America just as he inspired the implementation of fire departments in the new country.

As the fledgling country was feeling its way, Chicago became a bustling metropolis that needed a large fire department. The earliest documented history of the Chicago firehouse dog hails from two distinct photographs. The first known photograph of a Chicago firedog was taken in 1872, eight years after the Civil War and a short time after the disastrous Great Chicago Fire of 1871. Presumably, all information regarding firehouse dogs before the Chicago Fire was lost. Though the firedog tradition inevitably existed before this catastrophe, we were only able to locate information pertaining to dogs during the post-Chicago Fire era.

The earliest known photographs of firedogs were shot in 1874. The first is a formal portrait that has a black Lab in front of an old-time pumper and serious-looking firefighters in chairs. In the second picture, firefighters pose with their multi-colored mutt sitting on a Skinner Patent Hose Elevator rig. It is important to note that the two dogs in these early photographs were not Dalmatians.

Chicago had always been a melting pot of varying eth-nicities, and the Chicago Fire Department was no exception. The department employed men of many different heritages, and the Chicago firehouse dogs reflected this diversity. While the original firedogs in England were purebred, high-performing, well-trained canines, the dogs of the new America were not nearly from the same elite stock. In broad terms, America was still very young and extremely poor. The new fire departments could not afford to be as selective of its dogs.

The first real written or verbal account of a Chicago firedog was in the early 1920s. *Felix* continues to be discussed in firehouses and libraries today, making him the most legendary firehouse dog in the history of the department. The mutt rescued an entire engine company after finding an alternative exit for the firefighters when they couldn't escape a burning building. He also climbed ladders into fires and was credited with saving a baby. For those heroic deeds, his legend is recounted in the cement of his memorial at the Palos Hills Library in Palos Hills, Illinois.

Fifteen years after Felix, two Chicago firedogs were presented at the Chicago Charter Jubilee's first annual firefighters' tournament at Soldier Field. On Septem-

Black Labrador in front of Engine 1's crew (1870s).

ber 5 and 6, 1937, *Queenie* of Engine 125 and *Bruno* of Engine 2 demonstrated techniques used to assist firefighters when they traveled to fires.

In 1955, a reporter for the *Chicago American* newspaper spent several weeks covering Chicago's firedogs. The young reporter was Hal Bruno, who later went on to become Political Director of the ABC News Network and a lifelong fire department aficionado. Bruno's series was the most comprehensive analysis of Chicago firedogs to date and proved to be a crucial piece of Chicago history. While Bruno was covering a four-alarm fire in the Chicago Stock Yards, he noticed a group of dogs playing in puddles of water that formed in a vacant lot next to a burning warehouse. It was here that Bruno got the idea to do a series of articles and organize a contest to find the "best" firedog in Chicago.

It took several months to convince his managing editor, but in February, 1955, the project was approved. Bruno called each battalion headquarters to

Engine 1, 1874 — the earliest known photograph of a Chicago firehouse dog.

Unknown firedog on Engine 63 (1893).

Unknown firedog with the crew of Engine 19 (1910).

Unknown firedog on Engine 58's Boat Wagon (1900).

determine which companies had dogs, then set out with a photographer to research his story. He found 65 of the city's 142 firehouses owned a dog. Several houses had one dog for each company in the station. Suburban fire departments called to boast about their pets, so Bruno established a separate category for them. The reporter wrote a daily column that featured 65 Chicago Fire Department dogs and a dozen dogs from the surrounding suburbs over a three-week period in the *Chicago American.*

Bruno coordinated the contest at the Polack Brothers Shrine Circus in the Medinah Temple. The circus was eager to have the contest judged at one of their Saturday matinee performances, and the result was a capacity crowd with 12 finalists appearing before the judges on March 8, 1955. The 12 dogs were *Lucky* (Engine 18), *Chipper* (Engine 125), *Dottie* (Squad 2), *Bozo* (Engine 55), *Pepper* (Engine 27), *Nardi* (Hook and Ladder 3), *Hernando* (Hook and Ladder 39), *Mickey* (Engine 48), *Schnapps* (Engine 63), *Muggs* (Squad 3), *Sunshine* from Skokie, and *Streamer* from Batavia. Details of their stories and all of Hal Bruno's Chicago dog profiles can be found in subsequent chapters of this book.

Each dog was handled by a uniformed firefighter from his or her firehouse and presented to the matinee crowd by the ringmaster, Ross Paul. The contest was judged by Fire Commissioner Michael J. Corrigan and J.J. Shaffer, director of the Anti-Cruelty Society. Their final decisions were based on each dog's training as a firedog rather than appearance or pedigree. Corrigan explained, "[t]hey were all fine dogs, and the decision was close. But we agreed the honors should go to mascots who performed the greatest service to the firemen, and had the most experience." Along

with trophies, the city and suburban champs won a six-month supply of Rival Dog Food, and the finalists each received a case of the food.

The *Chicago American*'s champion firedog was Bozo the black-and-white terrier mix from Engine 55. Bozo's outstanding performance occurred on July 24, 1949, when he followed firemen into a burning building. Bruno explained that

> [a] small boy was reported missing in the dense smoke. Within minutes, the firemen heard Bozo's frantic barking, and found him with the nearly unconscious child in a smoke filled, second-floor bedroom. The boy was carried to the street and revived. Bozo was also responsible for training George, a deaf Dalmatian, who was mascot of Hook and Ladder 44 in the same firehouse.

A cheering section of kids from Bozo's North Side neighborhood were on hand to greet him when he stepped out on the circus stage, their applause rocking the Medinah Temple.

The second-place prize went to Lucky, the tough firehouse guard of Engine 18 and Truck 5, and Nardi, veteran mascot of Hook and Ladder 3 took the third-place trophy. Hernando of Hook and Ladder 39 was also awarded separately for saving the life of a robbery victim. The American Humane Association presented him with a bronze medal and the Anti-Cruelty Society's honor citation.

Streamer, a member of the Batavia Fire Department, was the suburban champion, yet another dog crowned for his demonstration of bravery—for ardently following his crew into fires. However, Streamer showed up late to accept his award because the Batavia firefighters went to a 5–11 alarm and allowed Streamer to roam too long at the scene. Streamer arrived covered in soot, but still took away top honors after final judging. Bruno also reported that Streamer's tail had previously been caught in the truck door.

The next time the alarm rang, Streamer turned his bruised tail to the truck and ran in the opposite direction. A few weeks later, the fire department purchased a new rig with an open cab and no doors, and Streamer went back to riding the trucks.

Following the contest, some of the finalists went on to become television celebrities. Several firedogs were featured on Curley Bradley's Animal Care Time television show on WNBQ–Channel 5. Dogs also appeared as guests of Win Stracke's Time for Uncle Win on WBKB–Channel 7. Bruno's story was a success and shed some much-needed light on an otherwise unknown side of the Chicago Fire Department.

Several months after the contest, dogs at two stations bit children, and Anthony J. Mullaney, who had just become the Chicago Fire Commissioner, issued an order that all fire mascots had to be chained and muzzled. Bruno recalled, "Squad 2 had a terrible time putting a muzzle on Dottie and leashing her to the deck gun for every run. They finally gave up and went through the agony of training her not to ride the apparatus. Similar depressing scenes took place all over the city as reluctant firefighters and confused dogs followed orders." Every firehouse around Chicago was subject to the rules of the commissioner and therefore barred from allowing their mascots to roam freely. Fortunately for the dogs, the rule was not in effect for very long.

The presence of the firedog permeates the Chicago Fire Department in other ways. For many years, the Mack Truck Company was the supplier of the city's fire apparatus. On every Mack Truck reigns a statue of a little Bulldog, and like the Dalmatian that led the way for the horse-drawn fire engines, the Mack Bulldog was always the first one out. Mack apparatus was phased out of the Chicago Fire Department several years ago, and no Bulldogs, either Mack or otherwise, can be found at present in a Chicago firehouse.

The Mack Truck Bulldog.

The 1991 blockbuster movie, *Backdraft*, a coming-of-age story about a rookie fireman in Chicago, was clear evidence that Chicago firefighters possess an image of superhero proportions. *Backdraft* demonstrated why firefighters are held in high esteem: They are men and women willing to give their lives to save others from seen and unseen dangers. The firedog character, *Thing*, was a Hollywood stand-in, inspired by the Chicago firedog, *Wino*, from Engine 83.

In the background of one of the *Backdraft* scenes, a painting was displayed at a retirement ceremony. A spin-off of the famous *Dogs Playing Poker*, the picture depicted a group of dogs playing poker in a firehouse, while the two dogs in the foreground cheat by passing cards to one another. In his work, simply titled *Dogs*, artist Lee Kowalski managed to capture the raw comedy that accompanies many firedog stories. Kowalski, a longtime fireman and painter of hundreds of different fire scenes, still considers *Dogs* one of his best and most humorous works. The presence of the painting in the movie provided an interesting parallel to the life of the firedog within the confines of the Chicago Fire Department—though not always center stage, the dog's companionship and loyalty are always felt.

The history of Chicago firedogs remains as rich as the cultural heritage of the city. Regardless of reputation, background, breed, personality, or performance on the job, they are all purebred Chicago firedogs. Cut from the same cloth and despite their differences (or perhaps because of them), they remain forever bound to the tradition of firefighting. One fact remains: wherever one finds a firehouse, he or she will likely find a firedog or a story of one.

"Dogs," by Lee Kowalski.

Chapter 2

The Life of the Chicago Firedog

⚜ The Life of the Chicago Firedog ⚜

Dalmatians earned their role in fire history and evolved into the mythic role of firehouse mascot. Though there is much truth in the association of firefighters and Dalmatians, Chicago firehouse dogs have not and will never fall into this stereotype. They have carved their own niche. They're more diverse, tougher, and their myriad traditions extend as far back as the first firefighters to work in the city. That the dog has evolved alongside human beings is a tribute to its steadfast loyalty and sense of duty to protect its master. The Chicago firehouse dog is no exception—the canines are more than best friends to the nearly 5,000 firefighters and other department personnel.

Firefighting is one of the Windy City's most cherished and noble professions. Battling everything from car fires to five-alarm blazes, these public servants risk life, limb, and sometimes their paws to protect the public. The relationship between firefighter and dog is mutually beneficial—they merge together as a single working unit, and though each plays a different role, both serve with unmatched fervor and impeccable dedication. The

That dog is more than a mascot—he finds the hydrant.

"That dog is more than a mascot—he finds the hydrant."

mascots are members of an exclusive sect of dog—those who dedicate their lives to service. While not sanctioned officers of the city, these canine warriors are no less a part of the fiber that comprises the department.

Chicago firehouse dogs are not usually trained to perform a specific job; that is, they generally don't attend obedience school, learn how to guide the blind down a street, or sniff out contraband in airports, but the services they provide are nonetheless valuable. The ways these dogs come to the firehouses are just as varied as their breeds. Firefighters frequently adopt a dog without the specific notion that they need one. Some dogs were rescued from scenes of fires; others just showed up at the firehouse door and never left. Some are donated by families, while others are a legacy, born on the very concrete floors where their parents served. Regardless of how they arrived, one ingredient is certain: the dog must be accepted by the entire firehouse—all three shifts. The animal's care is often entrusted to one firefighter who has forged a bond with the dog, but all the firefighters voluntarily assume responsibility for veterinarian, food, and upkeep bills. Because of this, the dog is equally shared among all the firefighters.

The duration of a dog's stay also ranges. Some dogs spend their entire lives in the firehouse. *Ashes* at Engine 29 continues to serve the house where she's been for the last 16 years. Other dogs are not as fortunate, lasting only a few short hours before being tragically killed by a car. Some run away or otherwise leave the firehouse because they

Brown Dog with some of the crew from Engine 52 (1965).

fire family. Chicago firedogs are rarely abused and, if anything, live a healthier existence than they would in the pound or on the street. You will read numerous stories of dogs that couldn't stay away from firehouse life; one even walked 30 miles from Des Plaines, Illinois, to get back to his crew.

Sometimes the firehouse dog is taken care of too well. Firefighters slipping a dog table scraps and leftovers after meals can result in quick

can't adapt to the unpredictable flow of firehouse life. One fireman took a dog home after it was discovered she was allergic to diesel fumes. Regardless of their term, unlike the firefighters, all firedogs are "on duty" 24 hours a day, seven days a week. Their only payment is the love given to them by their smoke-eating brethren.

Though the majority of local firedogs are originally unwanted or strays and face unique challenges living in a Chicago firehouse, they receive excellent treatment from their

and unhealthy weight gain for the dog, a practice now curbed by conscientious captains and firefighters who implement stricter feeding regimes for their pooches. Still, one firefighter summed up the fact of the matter, "The only skinny firehouse dog is a new firehouse dog."

While Chicago firedogs may receive better treatment in the firehouse, the flip side is that they are exposed to an increased risk of injury or death. In the 1950s, reporter Hal Bruno asserted, "by their own choice firehouse mascots

Engine 103's firedog guards the rig at the scene (1960).

often lead dangerous lives." It is not unusual for the dog to accompany firefighters into the fires, barking and sometimes even leading the hose teams to stranded victims. Sleeping on the same floor as the apparatus can be hazardous if the dog doesn't wake up in the middle of the night when the house gets a call—the rig won't stop to wait for a firedog to get out of the way. Certain neighborhoods of the city are more dangerous than others, especially when the dog is designated as the house's primary security system. *Rufus* of Engine 57 understood all too well the meaning of tough. After surviving nine car accidents, two shootings, and three stabbings, he remained a loyal, active-duty member of the department. And no firehouse in the city has a white picket fence to prevent their pet from running into the street. The general rule is that if a dog can survive the first year, it has learned enough lessons to make it through several more years without being hurt or killed.

Squad 5's logo.

Plush wall-to-wall carpeting is non-existent in a Chicago firehouse, so the dogs spend a majority of their time sleeping and playing on concrete floors. Because of this, they usually suffer from arthritis earlier in life, and their coats tend to get dirtier. Grooming is not a top priority. They lie on the oil-soaked ground day after day, and no matter how many baths they receive, they are rarely clean for very long. Depending on the dog, firefighters will warn others that their hands will become quite filthy, even black, from petting their dog.

Life on a firehouse floor comes with a price. There are countless stories of dogs requiring expensive surgeries and high-priced medications, even in old age. As there is no dedicated fund for these circumstances, all the firefighters of the house will chip in for medical care. But illness, no matter how grave, rarely stops the dog from trying to complete its call to duty. For example, *Brown Dog*, after 15 years of service, needed medication for arthritis. Even when taking several pills on a daily basis, *Brown*, as he was affectionately called, would howl until a fireman hoisted him into the front of the engine for a run.

Despite their ailments or age, the crew is always grateful for their dogs' dedication. One firefighter noted that even though he wasn't a dog lover when he was younger, living with Chicago firehouse dogs changed his view. "These dogs were given to us by God for a very important reason. They give you a lot of joy. There is a special type of bond that exists between the crew and their dog."

This bond is reinforced by the fact that many dogs ride the rigs with the firefighters as they respond to alarms. Since the beginning of their incorporation into firehouses, dogs have preferred to ride the engines rather than the hook-and-ladder trucks. Because the engines sit closer to the ground, they are easier for them to board and the various platforms more accessible. Engines are also the predominant piece of apparatus in the department's arsenal, almost every house has one. While most favor the engines, there is the occasional dog who does ride exclusively on the truck; some houses are lucky enough to have a dog for each.

Regardless of the rig, most dogs quickly learn the alarm codes that ring through the house from the 911 Center on the West Side of Chicago. Certain sounds indicate whether an ambulance is necessary, while others signify the need for an engine. If the alarm indicates a run for the ambulance, the dogs rarely move a muscle, but if the call for an engine comes over the system, they're on the rig well before anyone else in the firehouse. One firefighter commented that the dog actually improved the house's "push-out time" (the time between when the alarm sounds and when the rig leaves the house) because the dog barked ferociously until everyone boarded the apparatus.

A dog, eight pups, and three firemen from Engine 2 (1950).

Outside the firehouse, the dog also has a profound relationship with the surrounding neighborhood, especially with the children. Speaking of this bond, Hal Bruno wrote, "like most Fire Department dogs, *Princess* is also the mascot of neighborhood kids. She waits for them after school at the playground next door, and they walk, splash, and play with her. *Nardi*, in common with most fire station pets, is the idol of the neighborhood children, and often makes the rounds to

their homes." Because of children's fascination with the firehouse pooch, the dog is a focal point in educating them about the dangers of fire. When the dog speaks, children listen.

When the dog can no longer speak, firefighters are uniquely qualified to intervene, but the passing of a teammate is never easy. The most frequent cause of death for a firedog is not fire but the automobile. Many dogs are hit by cars when out playing or working in the streets. It's also not uncommon for the rig to run over the dog. Many are hit as the engine rolls out of the house; either the dog is too tired to move or too old to get out of the way. Rat poison has even claimed several dogs. Still, old age is also a leading cause, for it comes more quickly to the firehouse mutt than the domesticated housedog. Elaborate funerals are not unheard of and burials are typical, either in makeshift graveyards by the house or within the concrete of the house itself. Approximately half of the firehouses in the city have some sort of marker for a fallen dog. At Engine 95, there is even the "Tomb of the Unknown Dog"—representing all the unmarked plots for dogs buried along the backyard fences.

While the Dalmatian still remains a highly visible emblem of American fire departments, modern-day firedogs are no longer relegated to the margins of some Norman Rockwell painting on the *Saturday Evening Post*. And though some dogs may be composed of "57" different breeds like *Heinz* at Engine 83, contemporary dogs are as traditional as the brass poles that are shined in each of the Chicago firehouses. As one firefighter of an earlier era commented to the *Chicago Herald American*, although many of the dogs are mutts, "we consider them thoroughbreds."

Chapter 3

Legends of the City

⚖ Legends of the City ⚖

For every generation of firedogs in Chicago, there has usually been one outstanding dog that is distinguished in some fashion from its peers. These dogs leave an impact not only on the personnel they served, but also on the firefighters who never knew them. These stellar models leave an indelible mark upon their firehouses, and the mere mention of their names evokes fond memories and salty stories. Since the beginning of the twentieth century, three dogs have demonstrated such a supreme commitment to the Chicago Fire Department: *Felix*, *Bozo*, and *Caesar*. While Caesar symbolizes the modern age of the firehouse dog and Bozo represents the mid-1900s, Felix remains more than an icon of the earlier half of the twentieth century. He is a demigod among his firehouse brethren and stands alone as the dog that most influenced the Chicago Fire Department.

Cumulatively, these dogs are the heavy hitters. Inevitably, there will be debate on why we chose these three dogs. They may not have been the dogs with the most stories or the most pictures, but they are the dogs who embodied the ideal virtues of the firehouse mascot: loyalty, strength, faith, and duty. They are each legends in their own right, for they have endured the vagaries of time.

Felix

Felix was the Babe Ruth of Chicago firedogs. As one of the oldest and most legendary firehouse dogs in the Chicago Fire Department, he was a part of an elite group that went on every call, followed his crew into fires, and rescued lives. This common street mongrel inspired television specials, memorials, and remembrances for almost a century after his death. His firefighting colleagues truly considered Felix one of their own: a full-fledged Chicago fireman. Aside from the accolades of the department, the neighborhood adored him as well. Loud cheers for Felix could be heard when Engine 25 rushed down a street. Though the firehouse at Canalport Avenue and 22nd Street was torn down to make room for the Dan Ryan Expressway, his legend remains as strong as the monument that was built for him in the suburb of Palos Hills.

Felix was born in 1910; how he arrived at Engine 25 will forever be in dispute. Some say Felix was among a litter of seven abandoned puppies donated to a local tavern that later gave one of the puppies to a firefighter. One individual distinctly *Felix climbs to the rescue.*

remembers an injured Felix wandering into her father's local coal office, which later donated the dog to Engine 25. Perhaps it wasn't as complicated, and Felix was like any other stray dog that found his way into one of Chicago's firehouses. But exactly how Felix arrived at the house is not nearly as important as the legacy he left to the Bridgeport area and the city of Chicago.

When the injured Felix first hobbled into the house, the firefighters nursed him back to health. In time, Felix would more than

Felix preparing the engine for a run (1921).

repay the firemen for their kind acts. Felix Cinkosky was a repairman who worked out of Engine 25 and became the dog's primary caretaker. When the other men in the house needed something fixed, they called to Cinkosky, "Come here, Felix." The new dog also responded to the summons, and the name Felix stuck.

Felix grew to be a medium-sized mutt, mostly brown in color with some black and white patches covering his coat. Felix served the majority of his career with the horse-drawn fire engines, but he later became a part of history for a

widely circulated picture taken of him in 1920 aboard one of Chicago's first motorized pumpers. Judging from the photograph, Felix adapted well to the new type of apparatus. It was said that he made every run except one. On an off day, Felix wandered too far from the firehouse to hear the alarm, and when the firefighters returned, Felix was so ashamed that he couldn't bear to look at his comrades. It never happened again.

Like most Chicago firedogs, Felix learned the different "Waker" alarm bell sounds and would board the fire rig depending on the specific signal. As a result, Felix knew when the house had a run before the actual alarm rang and was always on the rig barking before the alarm finished sounding. But Felix did more than just go to work early.

Initially, Felix would serve as guard to the rig, not allowing anyone near it. As time wore on, however, he wanted to get closer to the action, and his duties greatly expanded. He learned how to climb ladders, making his way behind the firemen into the belly of the fire. Once

Felix inspecting the damage at a fire investigation.

der, Felix jumped on one of their backs, putting his front paws around the fireman's shoulders and his back legs tucked under his arms.

At one unusually intense fire, Felix followed the men into the flames as always, but the fire quickly overcame the two hose teams, and the fire outflanked the men. Because the path they forged with their hoses was no longer available, they had to find another way out of an extremely dangerous situation. Felix went to work. Through the smoke and flames, he left the firefighters briefly to look for a back entrance. After what seemed like hours, he came back barking ferociously. As one man held onto Felix's tail, he led the entire team on their knees out of the building. At the end of the day, all the men owed their lives to Felix.

Felix also had an uncanny ability to know if anyone was still in a burning building, and he refused to exit the scene of an active fire if people were still inside. On one run, the men of Engine 25 extinguished a fire and had begun evacuating the house. However, Felix went up to the porch door of the house, barking uncontrollably. After several minutes, the firefighters wondered why Felix was so focused on the house. Deciding to go back in for one more look, Felix led three firefighters directly to one of the bedrooms. Moments later, a fireman emerged from the charred house with a screaming infant in his arms.

Felix was so talented that P.T. Barnum from Barnum & Bailey Circus came to Engine 25 to see if he could perform. With his ability to climb ladders and unusual intelligence, there was no doubt he would have done very well in the show, but there was no way the firefighters were going to let him leave.

inside, Felix shadowed the men as they worked to extinguish the flames. When the firefighters went down the lad-

Felix also enjoyed the simple pleasures of the everyday Chicago firedog. He thrived on the attention from the local children who looked forward to giving him treats on their way home from school. Like most firedogs, Felix loved to eat, especially the liver sausage brought to him by adoring neighbors.

In 1926, Felix became the victim of a predicament common to Chicago firedogs; he was struck and killed by a car at the scene of a fire. While there were rumors of his dying from eating poison or too much liver sausage, Felix's long tour of service was recognized with Chicago Fire

Felix riding on Engine 25 (1920).

Department honors for dying in the line of duty. Felix was waked in the firehouse, surrounded by an elaborate $400 floral arrangement. A solid mahogany casket was donated by the owner of Karpen Furniture Company, J.B. Locke. It was handcrafted with such high workmanship that no nails were used in its production.

The entire neighborhood mourned the loss of their close friend. On the day of the funeral, all the schools in the neighborhood were closed so the children could attend the service. Six children, three boys and three girls, served as pallbearers. Tears streamed down their faces as they walked their friend to his final resting place. News media covered the event and took pictures for the newspapers. While televisions weren't yet popular, the Pathe News covered the story in the local theaters. Despite several attempts to locate these news reels, we were unable to recover them.

Eight automobiles and over 20 firefighters traveled from Engine 25 to the northwest corner of Kean Avenue and 95th Street where the wooden casket was interred. The chief of Engine 25 chose to bury Felix in the Palos Forest Preserve in the southwest suburbs—because it was on his way to his parents' home—and obtained a permit from the county commissioner to bury him there. A granite headstone donated by the Wunderlich Company reads "Felix No. 25. C.F.D."; there is no mention that Felix was a dog. To this day, people still bring flowers to his grave in gratitude for his service. Felix's impact had such a profound effect on the community that the residents coined an expression in his memory. Whenever they won at playing cards or a stick-ball game, adults and kids alike would exclaim that they had "won one for Felix."

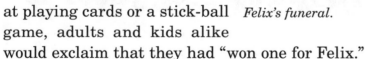

Felix's funeral.

The story of Felix did not end with his death. Around the time of his passing, Darlene Fillis was born. Years later, Fillis took an interest in the dog upon seeing a photograph of Felix's wake and dug deeper into the story. The spirit of Felix inspired the Palos Heights librarian to undertake a massive campaign to have a statue built in the dog's honor. Darlene and her daughter April sent out hundreds of flyers and news releases asking for support. But before a statue could be built, she had to find the dog's picture. She eventually acquired several photographs from two daughters of a fire captain, Patrick Collins, who had served with Felix.

Darlene received permission from the mayor of Palos Hills and the government board to proceed with the project. The Palos Hills Public Works Department helped out by supplying a cement pedestal for the monument. Through her vigorous campaign, she inspired the local community to give donations. Darlene attempted to obtain a grant for the project, but no one would provide her additional funding—she even had Felix's headstone on the front page of the local Yellow Pages. Still, the donations were hard to come by, and she was only able to collect $2,000.

The project, ultimately costing over $10,000 to complete, forged ahead with the support of Darlene's personal funds. Sculptor Michael Froding created the statue of the brave and devoted canine. After several years of hard work, the memorial was dedicated in a special ceremony on July 19, 1988. The 52-inch tall statue of Felix appropriately portrays Felix four times his size, as he was always larger than life. He still stands atop a 31-inch platform on a slope outside the Palos Hills Library—a proud memorial to Felix and the Chicago Fire Department.

Memorial statue at the Palos Hills Library.

Felix's headstone at 95th and Keane Ave.

Bozo

The pride of Engine Company 55, *Bozo*, will long be remembered for training a deaf Dalmatian and saving a child from the scene of a fire. These two acts won him the honor of "top dog" in the *Chicago American*'s firedog contest. Hal Bruno reported that Bozo was a hungry, lost puppy when he wandered into the house in 1947, but the mutt jumped aboard Engine 55 the second time he heard the alarm ring. A few weeks later, Bozo's rightful owner claimed him, creating unhappy firemen and an empty feeling in the house. Within hours of returning home with his owner, Bozo ran back to the firehouse, over four miles away. While the firefighters were touched, they reluctantly sent him back home to his master. When Bozo absconded again and returned in a few days, the owner told the lieutenant, "He goes wild when he hears a siren. Last night he chased a fire engine for two miles. I guess he'll never be happy anywhere else." So the owner relinquished Bozo to the firemen, and the scrappy Terrier mutt spent the next 13 years at the firehouse at 2740 N. Sheffield Ave.

Bozo ready to roll.

Bozo rode Engine 55 religiously, never missing a run; he was first on the rig, perching himself next to the driver, and frequently accompanied the men into the fires. One hot evening, while firemen were finishing up a basement fire, Bozo was a little winded and trotted into a nearby tavern. He found the bartender and tugged on his trousers until he was given a drink of water. Following the drink, Bozo raced back to the scene to guard the rig as firefighters were beginning to secure their equipment.

On July 24, 1949, Bozo's life as a "typical" firedog changed forever. Bruno reported that Bozo followed the firemen into a burning building at 652–54 W. Drummond Place. The fire was fairly large, but nothing the firemen couldn't control, and Bozo went running into the building well before the firefighters actually made entry. A small boy was reported missing to the fire chief, and the information was eventually passed to the firemen. Within minutes, the firemen heard Bozo's frantic barking in the dense smoke. Following the sound of his barking, the firemen quickly found Bozo lying next to a nearly unconscious child in a smoke-filled, second-floor bedroom. The boy was carried to the street and revived; the black-and-white mutt was a hero. A few days later, on behalf of a grateful city, Fire Commissioner Michael J. Corrigan presented the first of many awards to Bozo. The plaque hung in the firehouse until it was closed in 1966.

In 1955, six years after the rescue, Bozo appeared with 69 other candidates at the *Chicago American* fire mascot contest. He was selected as a finalist for the contest because of the rescue and for training his housemate *George*, a one-year-old deaf Dalmatian, to ride on Hook and Ladder 44. A cheering section of kids from Bozo's North Side neighborhood greeted him when he stepped onto the circus stage. The applause rocked the Medinah Temple, and Bozo was crowned the city's champion firedog. Along with an 18-inch high trophy, Bozo received a six-month supply of Rival Dog Food that was eventually shared with George.

Though Bozo behaved himself during the judging, the champ later decided he had received enough attention. Bozo slipped out of his collar and walked off the stage just as he was being led forward to accept the trophy. As Bruno described, "It was a trick he would live to regret."

In fact, it was almost the end of Bozo's career. When Commissioner Anthony J. Mullaney ordered all canines be chained and muzzled outside the firehouse, it was not met with happy firemen. However, for Bozo, a bad situation only became worse. On a freezing December night, at a 5–11 and two special alarm on the North Side, Bozo slipped out of his collar just as he did at the *Chicago American* contest. Bruno described it best:

Commissioner Mullaney spotted him trotting over the hoses as thirty-two engines, five hook and ladders, three squads, two water towers, two high-pressure wagons and 250 firefighters battled a roaring church fire. The Commissioner also roared and ordered a member of Engine 55 to remove Bozo from the fireground without delay. So an ice-coated firefighter tucked a struggling, wet terrier under his arm, *crossed out of the fire lines, hailed a surprised cab driver and escorted Chicago's champion firedog back to quarters.*

Bozo kept a low profile by staying out of trouble for the next five years and avoided an early retirement. He eventually reached an age where he had to be lifted onto the rig. A fireman would give him a boost onto the truck and he'd scramble over equipment to the front seat (Bozo always had to sit in front). Even then, he insisted on answering every alarm with the firefighters.

After 13 years of continuous service, Bozo was hit by an unidentified motorist shortly before midnight on a hot August night in 1960. Just as a good Samaritan came into the firehouse to let the firemen know the bad news, Bozo hobbled into the quarters under his own power and curled up in a back room. Everyone thought he was going to survive the accident until a couple of firemen noticed Bozo was missing the next morning. Bozo was found lying in the grass of the parkway across from the station; this time he couldn't make it home without help. The firemen got a stretcher from the firehouse and proudly carried their teammate home. A firefighter who retired a week earlier heard about the accident and accompanied his colleagues and Bozo on a trip to the veterinarian. The vet found Bozo's internal injuries too substantial, and there was nothing he could do except end his misery.

In September, 1960, Bozo's obituary was given an entire page in *Chicago Firefighter Magazine*. Bozo remained on the job throughout the tenure of three commissioners—he was the only firedog to withstand an order banning dogs in firehouses, and survived Commissioner Mullaney's personal vendetta against him as well.

Caesar

The arrival of *Caesar* into the fire department during the early 1970s is as illustrious as his years of service at Engine 22. A Playboy bunny, who was also a Playmate of the Month, dropped off the Dalmatian puppy at the firehouse. She was moving to Los Angeles and could no longer care for the dog. The firefighters of Engine 22 at 605 W. Armitage Ave. had an unusual fondness toward the dog, and Caesar's auspicious beginning was only a precursor to the life he would live over the next nine-and-a-half years.

As a puppy, Caesar was known for wandering the neighborhood, occasionally sneaking past the CTA's turnstiles to ride throughout the city on the elevated trains (he was not the only dog known for riding the "L" alone). Every time the dog went on the trains, a dutiful citizen who knew of Caesar's reputation returned him to the firehouse. Aware of Caesar's advanced social skills, the firefighters of Engine 22 often put him in a cab by himself and instructed the cabbie to drive to other firehouses with dogs. In return, the firefighters of the other houses would send their dogs by taxicab to Engine 22 to see Caesar. The crew from Engine 22 once called Engine 83 to arrange a visit because they heard that its mascot, *Wino*, was a female. The next day, a cab showed up with Caesar. He tried to woo Wino, but she was too much of a lady; Caesar came back rather dejected.

Caesar also made his mark riding the rigs to fires, following the men and women into battle, and being a tough enforcer of firehouse boundaries. Because of his love of the

Caesar from Engine 22.

engine, Caesar had his fair share of medical misfortunes. While defending the house against a would-be canine intruder, Caesar lost half of his ear when it was bitten off in the squabble. Still, he was a gentle dog that according to *Chicago Tribune* columnist Anne Keegan, "lost 1,001 fights and ran away from another 2,001."

Another episode occurred when a speeding car hit Caesar. The firemen quickly rushed him to a "human" hospital nearby, where the surgeon on duty sewed him up with 130 steel stitches and saved his life. However, the surgeon didn't match the dots on his coat correctly, and Caesar spent the rest of his days with one black dot cut in half. He was secretly returned to the firehouse covered in a white sheet on a stretcher so that no one knew that a dog was being treated at a non-veterinary hospital. The stretcher eventually became his bed, most likely because the hospital couldn't use it again and didn't want it back. Thanks to the firemen who administered the occasional IV tube and the several doctors who made house calls, Caesar healed quickly.

Caesar on top of the engine.

Caesar was also run over by an ambulance—actually, twice in the same day. In response to calls, the ambulance twice raced out of the house not knowing that Caesar was napping in front of the truck. Despite the harrowing afternoon, Caesar never missed a day of work, received worker's comp, or filed suit against the city. Though bruised and battered from the experience, he eventually recovered and stayed far away from the ambulance's path in the future.

Despite this slate of injuries, Caesar remained a permanent icon both in his firehouse and in the city, representing more than just the fire department. He was a symbol of the individual working firefighter, a constant fixture in the house. One of the firemen remarked that in the summers, as many as a hundred people a day would stop by the house in an attempt to meet the famous dog.

While fighting a fire at Armitage and Clybourn, a chunk of concrete fell on the engine, trapping a fireman. Keegan reported that at the hospital, a concerned nurse asked the injured fireman if Caesar was also hurt in the melee. Thankfully, he was not harmed. "That's Caesar," commented the fireman, "He's the most popular guy in the firehouse."

Caesar's celebrity was apparent on two distinct occasions when Caesar's eviction from the firehouse seemed imminent. The first occurred when neighbors complained that Caesar was traipsing too freely over their lawns in the middle of the night. The neighbors were also upset that the dog was a notorious bachelor. Thinking that the removal of the dog would bolster community relations, the commissioner ordered the dog's eviction. It would take more than a few offended neighbors, however, to terminate Caesar's commission. Persistent schoolchildren wrote letters to the commissioner, and the department, convinced that life was better with Caesar than without him, rescinded the order.

The second near-eviction occurred during the strike of 1980 when Caesar became the center of a political battle that again almost ended his tenure. The firefighters went on strike and took up ranks outside the firehouse, enduring the bitter cold that makes Chicago winters so famous. Loyal to his bosses and the union, Caesar also walked and took his place huddled underneath the blankets with the other strikers. On several occasions when his arthritis acted up because of the extreme temperatures, paramedics crossed the picket lines to bring Caesar back into the warm firehouse. Viewing this gesture as a threat, a young replacement lieutenant ordered the dog out, leaving Caesar to suffer with his comrades in the elements. At best, the order was a measure of revenge for the strikers. At worst, it was intimidation.

Engine 22's memorial for Caesar.

It was during the strike that *Chicago Tribune* writer Anne Keegan again took an interest in the pooch. After catching wind of the lieutenant's lack of concern, she used her column to honor Caesar and to broadcast how the dog was being abused as a political pawn to show the striking firefighters that insubordination would not be tolerated. Her article noted that "[Caesar] was always the first one on the truck, standing proudly up on the hose bed, his nose in the air, as the engine wheeled off down the street, siren screaming, heading for a fire. Often, he would follow his firemen buddies into the burning buildings to make sure they came out again." It also spotlighted a furious paramedic who gave the dog his medicine and injected him with cortisone shots. Willing to do anything, the paramedic maintained, "I personally will throw myself in front of the firehouse door. I'll handcuff myself to the dog—but I won't let him get thrown out." The emotionally charged "Close-Up" column produced more letters from outraged members of the community and those who saw the actions of the lieutenant as malicious and mean-spirited. Keegan's article proved to be Caesar's saving grace. Caesar was allowed to stay, and no "white shirt" ever attempted to get rid of the dog again.

The hard days of living at a firehouse caught up with the beloved dog. He slept more and more on his private stretcher and would go on runs only when up to the task. The paramedic who gave him his medical treatments finally took him to the vet and had him put to sleep. The bereft members of the squad erected a memorial outside the house that will remain as long as the building stands.

Chapter 4

North Side Firedogs

♨ North Side Firedogs ♨

Engine 125

One of the oldest firehouses on Chicago's Northwest Side is Engine 125 at 2323 N. Natchez Ave. Since 1917, this historic firehouse has seen the invention of the automobile, the first moon walk, and 16 presidents. More than that, however, the house produced one of the best firehouse dog stories in the twentieth century. Hal Bruno covered the 1950s tale of *Chipper*, the curly-haired cocker spaniel mascot who saved the life of a fireman.

Chipper was an animated dog, easily excited and known for his frequent bark. He relished the engine rides and, like most dogs, would stick his head out the window when the rig was screaming through the city. On a brutally cold winter night, Engine Company 125 responded to a violent fire. As always, Chipper accompanied the men into the flames, but this time the heat and heavy smoke became so intense the firemen were ordered out. Just as they reached the fresh air, the firemen noticed their pooch was missing. Without hesitating, the men delved back into the inferno to rescue their beloved companion.

When the firemen reached a smoky room, they found

Boots, perched on Engine 78.

a silent, weary Chipper hovering over an unconscious fireman who had collapsed from the smoke. Chipper remained calm and close to the floor, patiently awaiting the arrival of his crew. The firefighters quickly carried them both out of the burning building, emerging just before the remainder of the structure crumbled. Chipper resisted the natural instinct that every living creature has toward fire. Instead of fleeing, he saved a brother that night and, for his act of heroism, received a medal from the Rival Dog Food Company. He proudly wore the medal on his collar until the day he died and also went on to become a finalist in the *Chicago American* fire mascot contest.

Engine 78

Wrigley Field is one of the oldest professional baseball parks in the country. It exudes a certain charm that cannot fully be captured in words—though many have tried. Among the ivy, sunshine, and row houses with rooftop seating, there sits a tiny firehouse behind the stadium, known to all Cubs fans as Engine 78. When a homerun is hit out of the park over the left field wall, you can usually see the firehouse in the background as the television crew focuses on the fan who chased down the ball on Waveland Avenue. In between pitches, the WGN camera will sometimes pan to a shot of a single, stoic firefighter sitting next to a Dalmatian on the bench outside the house.

Engine 78 is a house steeped in tradition beyond its unique relationship with the ballpark. Amidst all the modern equipment the house shelters, Engine 78 still retains its horse haylofts from a bygone era. While there are no official records of the dogs at Engine 78, one can feel the spirit of countless canines who gave chase within its bricks. Among those was *Boots*, a dog so well-known and liked that she was incorporated into the house T-shirt design. Boots never forgot a firefighter who served at Engine 78. Anytime a former member came back for a visit or to substitute for a vacationing firefighter, Boots immediately recognized him. In the early 1990s, the captain of the station received Boots as a gift from the

Boots looking onto Wrigley Field with a friend.

local pet store. When the Dalmatian was a puppy, she slept on the captain's belly but eventually found a more permanent bed in a chair located in the living quarters upstairs.

Every morning, Boots wandered Wrigleyville, frequenting many local establishments, greeting neighbors and tourists alike. On one of her daily strolls, Boots returned with a wallet that she dropped in front of a fireman when she entered the house. The owner of the wallet lived next door, and the fireman promptly returned it. Interestingly, Boots took the wallet out of the neighbor's back pocket during a "friendly" visit.

From the Harbor on Belmont Avenue to the local Federal Express center, Boots had an impressive knowledge of Wrigleyville's side streets and alleyways. At Federal Express, the clerks gave her dog biscuits. In the afternoons, Boots usually snuck away to Murphy's Bleachers where she was a pro at scoring leftovers from the local lunch crowd. Boots's favorite spot, however, was that mecca for all dog owners and their pets—Doggie Beach, north of Belmont Harbor on the lakefront.

Like any good firedog, Boots rode on the engine. But there was one condition of her work: good weather. After the bell rang, Boots immediately stuck her head out the window of the house to determine if conditions were suitable for accompanying her bosses. If it was too cold, Boots usually decided to spend the day working as a guard dog rather than helping at the scene. Before the rig left, she always shot a glance to the firefighters, letting them know if she would be joining them. During the summers, however, she could always be seen on Engine 78.

Boots was also a diehard Cubs fan and a fixture at Wrigley Field, both in and out of the park. Like her 1970s predecessor, *Buster*, Boots gained free admission into Wrigley Field. During a game in 1994, she had the best seat in the house—on the field. Boots had figured out a way into left field via a parking lot entrance. After she charmed her way past security, it was a short walk from the door onto the green grass. Because none of the grounds crew could capture Boots, the captain personally came over to retrieve his mascot. Upon their exit, they received a standing ovation from the crowd. Boots was never found in the Friendly Confines again.

There's no place like home for Boots and Engine 78.

Following her debut as a Cub, Boots figured out a more practical way to watch the games. From the rooftops that line the outfield walls, Boots could be found partying with the other fans. She would sneak in with the crowds as they entered, and most folks enjoyed having her on the roof. Their admiration waned as she helped herself to the buffets and condiments. The firehouse was usually called to retrieve her around the fifth inning when the party started running out of food.

Boots was also known to chase the occasional home-run ball that hopped over the left field wall onto Waveland Avenue. On game days, when Boots was not at the park or on the rooftops, she could be found lounging at the firehouse. Kids would come over during the game and take pictures with her on the front bumper of the rig. Bachelorette partiers and VIPs often stopped by for a picture before the game.

During the winter season, Boots stayed behind to perform her secondary duties as a guard dog. She knew that as soon as the engine left the house, there was no one watching her. During these times, she would take a coffee break, which usually meant wandering the neighborhood. Eventually, these breaks became too frequent, and the firefighters had a difficult time getting her back to work.

During the Christmas season one year, the firefighters took Boots to a charity event that also featured Santa Claus. When she arrived, it was Boots who was the center of attention rather than Santa. The kids were more interested in playing with the dog than sharing their wish lists with the jolly fat man. Maybe it was because Boots was born on Christmas Day.

Boots served a full term at the house but was forced to take leave because of a medical injury. She had been run over by a car and was only able to use three legs. Her impediment slowed her a little, and she ultimately retired from the job when one of her beloved firemen took her home.

BOOTS WAS NOT the only Cubs fan in the firehouse. *Scotty* arrived in the late 1980s. Like any dog who lived across the street from one of the most popular ballparks in the country, he was an expert at networking, entertaining, and community relations. Extremely good-natured, he became a favorite with the young fans, beloved for his ability to charm a crowd. Perhaps it was the spirit of Ernie Banks or Ron Santo who inspired Scotty to play ball; he could catch a tennis ball as hard as anyone could possibly throw it. The spry mutt could easily capture lightning-fast pitches in his mouth, and fans lined up before and after games to watch Scotty play ball with the firefighters. Scotty was a master of safety, for he never chased the ball into the street. He would go all the way to very edge of the curb where the house's driveway met the street, but would never run into it.

In addition to his athletic skills, Scotty possessed a unique intelligence. He loved to cruise the neighborhood and knew to look both ways every time he crossed an intersection. Scotty also knew how to open the firehouse door to get back inside. He would reach up to the handle, turn it

Scotty, ready for action (1980).

with his paws, and let himself in. Firefighters would be chatting in the house and suddenly the door would open. Scotty would stroll back into the house, giving a look as if to say, "I'm home."

BEFORE SCOTTY, *Buster* also enjoyed baseball. He managed to sneak into Wrigley Field on more than one occasion, and the games were often stopped to return him to the house. He was the quintessential firedog—within a day of being at the house, he knew all the codes, and when an alarm sounded, Buster was the first on the rig.

Buster was killed in the line of duty one afternoon when he ran into a fire that began in the back of a building. The fire frayed some electrical wires and left them exposed in a puddle of water. Buster stepped into it and was immediately killed. The Associated Press covered the story, and as a result, Engine 78 received sympathy cards from all over the country and offers from numerous families willing to donate a new puppy to the firehouse.

KAREN KRUSE, AUTHOR of *A Chicago Firehouse: Stories of Wrigleyville's Engine 78*, reports that a similar incident occurred during the 1960s. *Spike* was a black Labrador known for leading the firemen into the blazes. There was a call to an elegant high-rise, and Spike ran wildly around the chic lobby while the men fought the fire. He snuck into the elevator to be with his team, but they had already returned home. Spike undoubtedly had a good time riding the elevators and romping throughout the building before making it back down to the lobby. Hours after the fire was extinguished, unaware that Spike had not returned with them, Engine 78 members received a call from the door-man sternly explaining that their dog was frolicking in his posh lobby. The firemen returned to pick up their mascot who was busy "sawing logs" on the couch.

Spike's hyper nature may have been his downfall, however. During a particular fire, Spike was leading the way down an alley and stepped onto a fence that was electrified by a fallen power line. He died on contact; the crew, now aware of the danger, deftly stepped around the fence. But for Spike, several firemen would have inevitably been killed. He was truly a hero.

ANOTHER ENGINE 78 MASCOT was *Pat*, a Spitz who rode the rigs to fires but always stayed on the engine. In the 1950s, Pat was the sentinel guarding post on top of the engine, protecting what he considered his property. If anyone came near the engine, he would snarl, flash his teeth, and send a clear signal that he owned the engine. Upon returning to the firehouse, Pat returned to being a serene, well-behaved dog. He would lie at the feet of the fireman who was standing watch and comfortably snooze away the afternoon.

Like all of the dogs who lived at 78, Pat was a Cubs fan. Hal Bruno reported that in the later innings (when the Cubs were doubtlessly behind), the ushers would let the firefighters into the park. Pat always accompanied them, without any guff from the ushers, and would some-how manage to successfully negotiate free hotdogs from the vendors who roamed the stadium. When the alarm sounded, however, he was still the first man on the engine.

Engine 30

The Chicago Fire Department's poster dog, *Thirty*, is a Dalmatian with piercing bright blue eyes. At six-months-old, he was donated to the house by two police officers who rescued him from several children who were abusing him. Engine 30 at 1125 N. Ashland Ave. voted to keep the energetic, untrainable puppy and named him after their engine. Since that first day nine years ago, Thirty has made over 14,000 runs and is on duty 24 hours a day, seven days a week, 365 days a year. As a collateral responsibility, he acts

Thirty riding along on the engine.

Thirty, preparing for a run.

as the entire fire department's mascot, constantly deployed for official functions. Whenever there is a parade or dinner, a department chauffeur picks him up at the house and drops him off at the event where he dazzles the guests with his exuberant charm.

Every time a call rings out over the loudspeaker, Thirty barks mightily and sprints toward the rig, waiting for the other members to come aboard. The doors to a fire engine are always left open for easier access during a run, and Thirty takes his place in the middle of the cab, always sitting right between the engineer and the officer on duty. Thirty is a master at handling the G-forces when the engine makes sharp turns at high speed. One firefighter likened it to watching a surfer hang ten on the waves of Hawaii.

When Thirty arrives at a fire, it's all business. While at the scene, he won't let anyone pet or play with him. He paces nervously around the perimeter, worried about his

friends, transforming back to his friendly self as soon as the firefighters are out of a building. He refuses to get back in the engine without his crew even if that means suffering icy paws in the winter. A fireman who was working a relief shift at Engine 30 recalls his first experience with the dog:

I was detailed to Squad 1, and we had a big fire near Chicago and Ashland where there was fire blowing out of the windows. So I grabbed my tools and mentally prepared myself, as this was only my third full-blown fire. I was very focused and very intent on the job at hand, and as I walked by Engine 30 (which was maybe 50 feet from the building), Thirty barked VERY LOUD right at me. I was mentally prepared for an explosion, a back-draft, a flashover, or a building collapse, but I was NOT ready for a Dalmatian to bark right in my face. I didn't even know Engine 30 had a dog, much less a dog that made the rig. I looked over at this snarling, barking beast while still walking towards the fire. I took my eyes off the street

Thirty in front of his rig.

and tripped over Engine 30's charged hoseline, falling almost flat on my face and skinning my knee, right in front of my lieutenant, two battalion chiefs, and a deputy district chief.

When the firefighters are finished fighting the fire and are cleaning up a scene, Thirty explores the neighborhood. All it takes to get him back is a single toot of the engine's horn.

Back at the house, Thirty is used mostly as a guard dog. With the help of a mannequin dressed in firefighter's regalia named "Tank," Thirty keeps the vagrants away with a loud tirade of barks. He needs to be near people during every waking moment, and whenever the firefighters are standing around in the house, he will nuzzle underneath their legs and stand patiently, waiting for affection. He is known for one trick that he still performs despite his age. While offering a treat, the men coax Thirty into excitedly jumping up and down; then he hesitantly rolls over and is rewarded his just desserts.

Thirty has made the news several times. He's been in countless photographs in both the *Chicago Tribune* and *Sun-Times* and has made numerous appearances on local television stations. One story in particular didn't make the cut. While the men were waiting to receive orders to return home, Thirty was running around the scene rambunctiously. Many reporters were there covering the intense blaze. An anchor from one of the network news stations was interviewing a witness—in a skirt. Needing to nuzzle in between the closest person's legs, Thirty went up to her and stood right underneath her. The consummate reporter remained calm, and the only sign of shock was her raised

eyebrows. She continued to go along with the interview trying to ignore Thirty's need for attention.

D<small>URING THE</small> 1950s, Engine 30's *Butch*, a Boston Bulldog, was among the ugliest members of the department and the

Rex relaxing on the hose (1988).

easiest to get along with. Hal Bruno quoted a fireman as saying that Butch "has proved beyond a shadow of a doubt that he is not a spectacular, brave, or smart dog. But for plain, old shoe comfort, we'll take our little Butch in preference to all those heroic paragons of dog-dom— and count our blessings." Engine 30 was also home to *Rex* in the late 1980s. The mutt was a bit of a misfit however, and for some strange reason never left the basement.

Engine 27

Pepper of Engine 27 at 1244 N. Wells St. accompanied his crew to every fire without fail. Though riding the rig is not unusual in itself, Pepper's actions at the scene gained notoriety during the 1950s when Hal Bruno wrote of his behavior in the *Chicago American*. Immediately after the engineer stopped the rig, Pepper jumped off and eagerly searched for the nearest hydrant. Once found, he barked incessantly until the men began installing the hose lines. If the men didn't use the plug Pepper chose, he growled in disapproval.

While most dogs yearn for the nearest fire hydrant in their daily walks, Pepper's ability to seek out the hydrant did not stem from an urge to relieve himself. The intelligent pooch learned the maneuver from watching the "hydrant man" open the plug. Pepper's ingenuity was greatly appreciated when the men needed to find a hydrant, but if the crew was responding to a false alarm, they had to tear Pepper away from the plug and forcefully put her back on the engine. His actions merited a spot in the finals in the *Chicago American* contest.

Engine 4

Surrounded by high-rises, Engine 4's quarters at 548 W. Division St. appear out of place, looking like a tiny shack in the neighborhood of Cabrini Green. The most notorious housing projects in the United States border the Gold Coast, one of the most prestigious neighborhoods in the country, and the engine and truck are constantly called into action in both areas. It has always been a tough neighborhood. Driving along Division Street, you can see evidence of the firefighters' work: smoke-stained brick and boarded up windows from fires that began in the higher floors of the public housing units.

Understanding this neighborhood is crucial in comprehending the grit of these dogs. Burglars routinely prey on the house, hoping to ransack the property. When firefighters leave for a run, the house is vulnerable to attack, and the dogs often remain behind to protect the house. It takes an intense kind of dog to remain vigilant when the firefighters are nowhere to be found.

The most famous of the dogs that served with the fire-fighters of Engine 4 was *Bear*. A mutt with a touch of Lab, Bear was sheathed in black fur and completed his tour of duty during the mid-1980s. One of Bear's greatest loves and most honed hobbies was his ability to hunt rats. Every time he dropped the carcass of the dead rodent, he was rewarded with a bowl of ice cream.

Behind the firehouse, there was a chain-link fence where Bear made his home. Unfortunately, one afternoon, a group of young kids lured Bear over to where they were standing and pinned him up against the fence. They then commenced a brutal assault on the dog; so brutal that Bear had to be taken to a local hospital. His left hind leg was so badly mangled that it needed to be amputated. Then-mayor Jane Byrne, who made headlines when she spent one month in a Cabrini Green apartment, contributed $700 from her political fund for Bear's operation. After the successful surgery, the house made dinner for the mayor to thank her for her generous donation.

Bear enjoying a treat (1980s).

Bear eventually adapted to having only three legs, still riding the rigs and jumping into the firemen's laps. He became famous throughout the city, known simply as the "three-legged dog."

It was through his favorite toy, a rubber handball, that Bear met his untimely demise. While playing a game of fetch with one of the

Bear hopping along on three legs (1980s).

department members, Bear choked on the ball and subsequently passed away. He was cremated and his ashes were kept in a Folgers coffee can on a shelf in the kitchen. To honor Bear's service, the men and women of Engine 4 had a brass plaque constructed that read: *Bear, the True Mascot of the Members of Engine 4 and Truck 10*. They fittingly nailed the plaque to the firehouse wall with only three bolts.

BEAR WAS FOL- LOWED by a pedigree Belgian long-haired German Shepherd named *Eddie*, who gained fame for his superior ability to balance himself in the middle of the hose bed while the truck took sharp turns at high speeds. In the 1980s, *Tower*, another large German Shepherd, served at the house and was known for going into the fires. A Dalmatian by the name of *Cleo* was Engine 4's mascot in the 1970s.

Engine 20

Max was a hefty, one-eyed German Shepherd famous for riding on Engine 20, 1320 W. Concord Pl., when it was called out on a run. Max never stayed on the engine while the men battled the blaze. When "leading out" at a fire, Max grabbed the hose in his mouth and helped the guys pull it off the hose bed. Occasionally, he would accompany the men into the fires, finding his way in and out of the fires by the hose lines that extended from the engine or a hydrant.

On one occasion in the 1970s, Max followed a group of firemen who went into the fracas without a hose because they were trying to rescue a stranded victim. Being in the middle of a burning structure is absolute chaos and, without the hose lines in place to guide Max, he was left to the mercy of the smoke. Firefighters outside the structure were spraying the building and water naturally began accumulating—always a dangerous thing because the electricity from a live wire can create a deadly puddle. Max acciden-

Max on Engine 20 in front of the house (1970).

Maxine and Max posing for the yearbook.

tally stepped into one of these pools, and the shock coursed through his body.

Upon exiting the building, a fireman noticed Max lying in the pool. After ensuring the wires were secured, a fireman immediately began CPR and chest-compressions in an effort to revive him. The process worked, and Max's heart began pumping again. Though tired and aching, Max came back to life and lived out the rest of his days following hose lines, a little more careful each time he left the engine.

Max's display of heroism in dutifully following the firemen was so compelling that it made the front page of the *Chicago Tribune*'s Sunday magazine:

> [I]n Chicago fire stations today, rookies like 12-month-old Max, Midwest's cover dog today, spend most of their time playing with squeaky toys, running in the yard, teething on dog candies, and being petted by 30 firemen. At the end of a busy day, Max curls up in a phone booth and closes the door, so he won't have to sleep in the dark.

Max died years later in the line of duty. He loved to follow the rig, even if they were just going to wash it. On this particular day, Max didn't see where he was in relation to the firehouse door and got his head pinched in the door jam. If he had his other eye or if he was younger, he probably would have made it out. His injuries were too severe, and Max was buried in the back of the house. His memory lived on in other dogs, for his successors were named *Max II* and *Maxine*.

Snorkel Squad 1

The firehouse for Snorkel Squad 1, in the heart of the Cabrini Green Housing projects at 1044 N. Orleans St., has since closed. But the toughest neighborhoods often produce the most intriguing and enduring stories. The dogs of Snorkel Squad 1 were a necessary tool in ensuring the safety of personnel and property in the maze of high-rise complexes. Despite the stray bullets and widespread crime, the house managed to generate a rich firedog tradition.

The story of the dogs that lived at Snorkel Squad 1 begins in the 1960s with a Saint Bernard named *Omar*. He was a product of the world-renown Von Saeuliamt family of Saint Bernards from Zurich, attributed with perfecting the exceptional qualities of the indigenous breed. As a puppy, Omar served as an ambassador aboard Swiss Air's inaugural flight from Switzerland to Chicago. As a sign of appreciation and goodwill, the government of Switzerland gave Omar to Mayor Richard J. Daley following the transcontinental flight. In turn, the Mayor gave Omar to Commissioner Quinn, who then gave him to Snorkel Squad 1.

Reaching over six feet tall when standing on his hind legs, Omar ranks among the largest dogs ever to serve in the department. Because of his enormous size and rugged good looks, Omar became one of the only "official" fire department mascots, representing the city at countless functions.

As a pure Saint Bernard, he made a handsome statesman, and when marching in parades, all eyes were on him.

The Chicago Fire Department Band used Snorkel Squad 1's quarters to practice for upcoming events. As a

Omar arriving from Switzerland, before he joined the department (1962).

puppy, Omar was constantly around the band and developed a certain affinity for the instruments and their players. The band members encouraged Omar to lead them in every parade and dressed him for the part; if he were marching in the St. Patrick's Day Parade, Omar was decked out in green. Whatever the occasion, Omar was the leader amidst the clashes of the drums, the whiny hum of the bagpipes, and the ringing of cymbals. And no matter the function, he always had his oak brandy keg around his neck. He was, after all, a purebred firedog with a strong Swiss heritage.

Though the press covered every official Chicago Fire Department event, there were two parades that received unusual media attention. The first took place in 1965 at the inauguration ceremonies for President Lyndon B. Johnson in Washington, D.C. Wearing an LBJ hat and displaying his keg, Omar marched in the parade with the department band past the new president. Unfortunately, the dog ignored presidential protocol. The *National Enquirer* and *Life* magazine gossiped that Omar gave LBJ's dog, *Yuki*, the "cold shoulder." The president's dog was a tiny mutt, and the pedigreed Saint Bernard showed little interest in her. The next year, the band was invited to march in the Rose Bowl parade in Pasadena, California. Omar's presence in front of the Chicago Fire Department Band brought fame from coast-to-coast, and the well-cultured pooch became a national symbol of good will.

After the presidential snub, there was some good-humored speculation by the gossip columnists as to why Omar would insult the Texas Democrat's dog. As it turned out, the reason for the "snub" was because of a dog named

Zellie. She too was brought over by Swiss Air a few years after Omar. In May of 1965, the two were married in Snorkel Squad 1's house. The ceremony was complete with a veil for Zellie and a vanilla wedding cake, which the couple quickly devoured. The *Chicago Tribune Magazine* even reported the event. Following their marriage, they wasted no time in having a litter of puppies. The firehouse kept one of the puppies to carry on his father's line at the house and named him *Zimm*. But like many marriages, it wasn't perfect, and the *Tribune* reported rumors that Omar "corresponded secretly with *Bernice*, a Saint Bernard from Wisconsin."

Omar could instill fear into the hearts of brave men merely by his enormous size. He was so large, in fact, that he had to be groomed in Snorkel Squad 1's shower. In front of children, he proved to be the gentlest of giants, but if a grownup dared cross him, Omar raised one of his lion-sized paws and slapped at the ill-favored person.

Whenever the refrigerator door opened, Omar mechanically ran into the kitchen and waited for some leftovers to fall to the floor. One afternoon, a police officer came into the house to visit a fireman and brought along his K9 police dog that, like most such dogs, was trained to fight. The cop went to the fridge and threw a hambone on the floor for the K9. Omar raced into the kitchen and, upon seeing the hambone in the K9's mouth, slapped it away with his big paw. The K9 went running into another room. If dogs could smile, Omar would have as he chewed on the bone. The police officer dejectedly left the house, frustrated that his K9 couldn't keep pace with Omar. After the cop left, the firefighters couldn't help but laugh.

Near the end of his reign, people from all over the country who magically knew of Omar's fame came to 1044 N. Orleans St. to have their picture or their child's picture taken with him. While his mammoth size prevented him from riding the rigs, he fulfilled his duties as a Chicago Fire Department statesman, bandleader, and protector of Snorkel Squad 1.

Omar, LBJ's biggest fan (1965).

OMAR'S SON ZIMM was affectionately referred to as *Zimbo*. In the 1970s, he carried on his father's responsibilities as firehouse guardian and, like his old man, led the band in their parades. Zimm looked like his dad but wasn't nearly as big. However, he took the role of pageant leader and modified it. Yes, he wore the St. Patrick's Day getup for

Omar leading a parade (1964).

the parade, but he was also known for donning a firefighter's helmet, cowboy hat, and fez. When he wasn't marching in parades, he followed his father's lead by hanging out at the house and staring down anyone who looked out of place.

TIMES HAD CHANGED since the Omar days, and the firehouse needed a dog that could protect the men from more than fires. During the late 1970s, statistics showed that the area around the house was, per capita, the leader in crime across the country. The neighborhood was a war zone. Two Chicago police officers were shot and killed a few feet from the firehouse door. *Fritz* served in the same manner as the police officers who frequented the house.

His comrades described Fritz as "The Boss," "The Bodyguard," or "The Man." Fritz was donated as a puppy from a breeder who was a friend of a firefighter at Snorkel Squad 1. From the very beginning, Fritz never feared the area, and no firefighter dared walk the neighborhood without him. Fritz was a purebred, black Belgian Shepherd who knew how to throw muscle around when needed. The "tough" kids

Omar, Master of Ceremonies, and Snorkel Squad 1 (1964).

kept their distance when Fritz was outside. They could even hear his roar as high as the twenty-sixth floor of the buildings that surrounded the house. The firefighters who lived there noted that Fritz was better to have around than police officers, because the local residents were more afraid of the mid-sized dog than the gun-toting cops.

Fritz also kept the neighborhood honest. He once cornered five teenagers who were ditching school. In an attempt to flee Fritz, the kids climbed to the top of a ten-foot fence that surrounded one of the parks. Unable to escape or climb down the other side, the teenagers were stranded. (These were the same kids who frequently threw rocks at Fritz when dusk set in.) A firefighter came to the rescue and made them individually apologize directly to Fritz before calling him off, but not before Fritz walked them back to class.

Fritz also knew who belonged in the house and who did not. He slept with everyone in the bunkroom and fiercely protected them. There wasn't one person who came into the house who didn't first receive a security review by Fritz. The dog had such a vicious reputation for only recognizing his crew that every battalion chief who picked up morning reports at the house didn't dare come in. Every morning these senior officers waited outside the house for someone on duty to deliver the necessary paperwork. They never came in because they didn't want to deal with Fritz's shakedown at the door.

He was not mean for the sake of being mean, but if threatened, Fritz defended himself. Firemen said that every person who was on the receiving end of a Fritz bite deserved it. Every time he bit someone, the firefighters were required to take Fritz to the Lakeshore Animal Hospital to ensure he didn't have rabies. The hospital kept him for a night and sent him home with a clean bill of health. On one occasion, he bit a person who was taunting him with an iron pipe. After that episode, none of the firefighters could find him. They went for a drive and found him sitting on the front porch of the Lakeshore Animal Hospital with a very guilty and knowing look on his face, waiting for his night of incarceration.

One evening, Fritz was waiting in the back of one of the firefighter's cars on a supply run. The car had tinted windows, making it nearly impossible to see inside. This proved to be unfortunate for a teenager hoping to steal the radio. As the teen was attempting the break-in, Fritz somehow knew a bark would blow his cover and remained quiet. The burglar managed to unlock the door. Just as he sat down to begin work on the radio, Fritz pinned him to the back of the seat. Moments later, the firefighter arrived. They made a brief pit stop to the local police station prior to getting the groceries back to the house.

Fritz served at Snorkel Squad 1 for over 12 years. He eventually was overcome by hip dysplasia and put to sleep. There wasn't one firefighter who served in Snorkel Squad 1 during Fritz's tenure that didn't appreciate the necessary service he provided. They always felt safe sleeping in the quarters because of his presence. Fritz may not have the most spectacular résumé—he didn't save babies from a torrent of flames and didn't follow firefighters into burning buildings. But he saved lives every day he was on patrol through his uncommonly common duty to protect his colleagues from the dangers of the city.

Engine 11

Engine 11 was located on the north edge of the Loop, steps away from famous Chicago landmarks and the "Magnificent Mile," the lush strip of luxury condos and upscale stores on Michigan Avenue. The area is also a political hub, home to several international consulates and dignitaries. Though Engine 11 on 10 E. Hubbard St. eventually moved to North Cumberland Avenue, one story of its pet Bulldog in the 1960s continues to be told and retold in neighborhood bars and gathering spots throughout the city.

In 1959, the crew from Engine 11 was called to a massive fire at the British consulate on Rush Street (which has since been moved to an office on Michigan Avenue in the Wrigley Building). The men of Engine 11 acted quickly, extinguishing the flames in record time and saving vital papers, artifacts, and records. The foreign officials were so impressed with the firefighters' diligence that they decided to reward them with a genuine English gift.

Opting against a lifetime supply of tea and crumpets, the consulate preferred to donate a lasting remembrance,

Unknown dog and fireman gazing out of Engine 11's house (1960).

one that would remain a perpetual reminder of their gratitude and appreciation. The consulate delivered *Butch*, a brown-spotted, purebred English Bulldog from a breeder in London, marking the first time the Chicago Fire Department ever received a dog in exchange for their performance at a fire. The English consulate, along with several excited firefighters, picked up their imported gift at O'Hare Airport. The dog adapted quite nicely to firehouse life, doing a lot of eating and sleeping, but never quite mustering the energy to jump on the rig.

Each winter, when the snow was over Butch's head, the dog pooped wherever he had the urge. The firefighters couldn't clean it up because it melted into the snow too quickly. However, the spring thaw revealed more than just wet sidewalks and old-looking grass. By April, the firefighters' favorite sport was watching the pedestrians play hopscotch between Butch's remnants, often betting on who would step on one of the landmines. After living in the house for only two years, Butch died of a heart attack while in the "throws of passion."

Engine 22

Engine 22 at 605 W. Armitage Ave. was the home of the legendary firedog *Caesar* (see pp. 40–42). Caesar's status as a big roller among firedogs, however, did not eclipse his predecessor, *Bear*. Not to be confused with the three-legged Bear at Engine 4, this one from the 1970s was a massive, black Newfoundland who reached a weight of over 200 pounds. The Newfoundland breed, or "Newfies," descends from the Canadian province with the same name. Raised as fishing dogs, the breed is among the largest, yet most gentle.

Bear could grip a fully inflated basketball in his mouth, and the men would frequently play catch with a basketball rather than the standard tennis ball. Because the size of a basketball is a little larger than a man's head, the firefighters got the bright idea to test whether they could fit one of their own heads into Bear's mouth. One of the men succeeded, much like a lion tamer would do at the circus. He came up with hair full of dog drool, however, and unlike a lion tamer, did not receive thunderous applause. Instead, furious laughter and continuous urges to repeat the stunt came from his comrades.

DURING THE 1950s, Engine 22 and Squad 10 were located at 522 W. Webster Ave. The house was home to a Dalmatian named *Chi-Chi* who mothered a litter of puppies every couple of years. Many of the puppies grew up to become firehouse dogs just like their mother. One of her offspring, *Shoes*, became the mascot at Engine 33, located at 2208 N. Clybourn Ave.

Engine 124

In the 1970s, the *Chicago Tribune* reported that *Sparky* from Engine 124, 4426 N. Kedzie Ave., had to be retired early because of an allergy to diesel fumes. After the retired wirehaired Terrier went home with one of the officers, a concerned citizen dropped off an abandoned dog at the firehouse. The crew named the tiny, shaggy-faced mongrel *Whiskers*.

Her zeal for public service was unparalleled. As one firefighter put it, Whiskers "took to life in the firehouse like she had been born into it. She has her favorites, but she likes all the men and even won over some of the grumpy ones." At the time, Whiskers was known as the smallest dog in the department and often slept on the coats or in the boots of her favorite firefighters. Although she was small as firehouse dogs go, she was deft in her moves and never got in the men's way. She was too tiny to jump on the rig like the other dogs, but Whiskers usually received help from a firefighter and rode to the fires in the cab of the engine. The men dubbed her "the official greeter" because the happiest part of her day was when she was able to meet the new shift coming to work in the morning.

During the firefighters' strike of 1980, the men of Engine 124 huddled in the warmth of Heinzel's gas station across the street from the house. Whiskers naturally hung out with them. When the firefighters finally got a contract and the strike was over, they all returned to the firehouse. Well, almost everyone. Whiskers was apparently not happy with the contract and never returned to the house. She lived the rest of her life in the gas station.

BARNEY CAME INTO the house after Whiskers refused to return. Every so often, the cook of the house prepared an unusually extravagant meal, and Barney always had a place reserved at the table. During one such occasion, the main course was filet mignon, and the district chief happened to visit the house just as the meal was being served. There were 13 filets, and the chief complimented the cook on the wonderful aroma and appearance of the steaks as he sat down in front of an empty plate. "Who's the extra one for?" the chief asked. "Barney," the firefighter replied. The stout officer laughed and began tucking a napkin under his neck. The fireman placed the extra filet on the plate in front of the chief and began cutting it up. "You don't need to chop it up for me," the chief said, grinning from ear to ear. When he finished cutting, the cook whistled and called Barney's name. Barney slowly came walking over from his corner as the firefighter put the plate down on the ground, and Barney began

Barney with his rig (1982).

Barney's yearbook picture (1988).

eating the carefully prepared steak. The district chief threw the napkin down and stormed out of the firehouse. The cook looked at his fellow firefighters who were laughing hysterically and said, "I told him it was for the dog."

On a vacation day, Barney tried hunting in the woods with one of the firefighters. He didn't last long, running for cover as soon as a shot was fired. The fireman looked for hours and later called the firehouse to tell them that Barney was missing and probably gone forever. The hunting party started a bonfire later in the evening and lamented their loss. As the fire started to roar, they could hear Barney in the distance barking. He had been huddled under a nearby bush since the original shot. Barney used these same concealment techniques in his days of hiding under the bar of the local pub. Then it was not because he was frightened, but because he was having too much fun and never wanted to call it a night.

Barney's knack for having to be rescued was his stock-in-trade. He had been missing from the house for a couple of days when a firefighter spotted two girls walking north on Kedzie Avenue with a dog on a rope. The dog looked exactly like Barney. The firefighter asked the girls their dog's name. They responded, "Sam," but when the firefighter pointed out to the girls that the tags clearly said "Barney," the girls

replied, "I knew we shouldn't have taken him." Barney was happy to be back again.

Barney always rode the rigs. On one occasion, he fell off and broke his leg. Despite his pain and the squawking of the men to stay at the firehouse, fearless Barney knew no other way of life and continued to ride. When Barney died, the firefighters spent several hours cutting out the cement of the apron to serve as a gravesite. As such, Barney is honored every time Engine 124 rolls out of the house.

IN THE EARLY 1990s, a mutt who wandered into the house as a puppy caught the name *Striker*. Still guarding the house today, he is a true city dog, for Striker hates grass and refuses to walk on it. Like any member of the Chicago Fire Department, he has developed a deep protective sense for his colleagues.

Several years ago, there was a fire at a house directly behind Engine 124. The firefighters responded by running hose across the alley to the burning house. An interested motorcyclist was driving dangerously up and down the alley checking out the fire. Striker saw the obvious distraction to

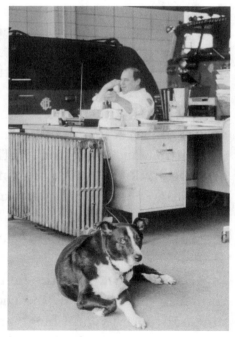

Striker standing post at Engine 124's desk.

the firefighting efforts and made a point to end the interruption. It only took Striker a few seconds to chase the motorcycle down the alley and into the street. The biker got the message and never returned.

Engine 13

If there was ever a dog that would fit well within a state governor's mansion or the White House, *Lucke* is it. He is the firehouse dog who accompanies his owner, Maureen Skorek, to work on the second shift at Engine 13, 259 N. Columbus Dr., Lucke occasionally rides the new rig but usually prefers to hang back at the house. At night, he sleeps in the bunkroom with Maureen.

Presidential candidate Al Gore came to Chicago in August of 2000 to campaign with the Chicago firefighters. Because Lucke could literally "smile" by raising his lips, he was inevitably a charmer with the press. No tour would be complete without a firehouse visit, and the dozens of reporters who accompanied Gore snapped a photograph with the candidate in front of Engine 13's classic red fire engine, complete with the black-spotted Lucke.

The Chicago Firefighter's Union reported in their newsletter, *The Sounder*, that

> [w]ith wife Tipper and daughter Sara along, Gore chatted with members and even met Lucke, the firehouse Dalmatian. Lucke's quite a ham, it seemed, and his owner FF Maureen Skorek did a great job of keeping Lucke awake after she started dozing in the sun on the apron. Gore seemed more impressed with the dog than

anyone, and couldn't resist making sure his wife heard the dog's name. 'His name is Lucke,' he said with a grin.

When not schmoozing with would-be presidents, Lucke donates his time with Skorek by attending fire safety presentations for youngsters at area schools. But don't try to feed him tomatoes. On a particularly slow afternoon, the house decided to grab some submarine sandwiches for lunch.

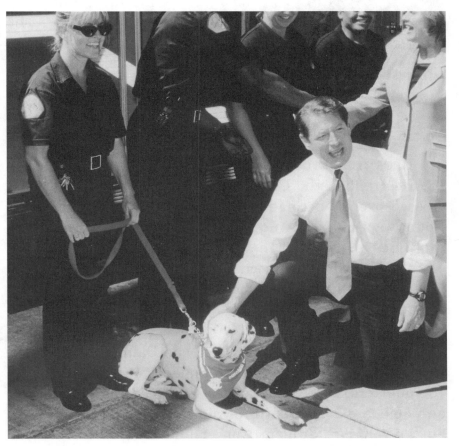

Lucke and Vice President Al Gore.

Lucke jumps for Al and Tipper Gore.

Skorek volunteered to go and took Lucke along for the ride. She returned with the food, placed it in the car, and then stopped for soft drinks. Lucke was left alone with the subs for only a few minutes, and when Skorek returned, she found empty wrappers scattered all over the car. The only remnants of food were the tomatoes Lucke declined to eat.

RECENTLY-RETIRED *MOSES* is another dog from Engine 13. He climbed the Chicago firefighting ranks and then crossed over to become a search-and-rescue dog for Cook County, specializing in collapsed building searches. Moses continues his work for the Chicago Fire Department in the city's public education sector. He usually rides an antique rig to local schools, where he educates children on the hazards of fire.

IN THE LATE 1950s, there was one Dalmatian who captured the praise of Flying Man Squad 1, located at Engine 13's quarters on 209 N. Dearborn St. No fireman could work over 56 hours in a week (three nights in a seven-day period), but *Lady* was a diligent worker and refused to obey the order. Lady knew the clicks of the "squawk box" better than

any dog in the department and guarded the rig at fires. Nobody except a fireman from Squad 1 could even touch the rig when Lady was around. One morning, on the way home from a fire, the crew stopped by Grant Park to let Lady get some exercise. She jumped off the rig and was completely overwhelmed because it was the first time she had ever felt grass underneath her paws. Eventually, the firehouse decided it was time for her to retire. Lady was becoming too old for firehouse life, and they needed to find a new recruit.

BLANCHE OSBORNE, A member of the Chicago American Soldier's Friends, helped the men of Engine 13 find a replacement. Many World War II veterans traveled to this association seeking help in getting back on their feet. While there, they sometimes suffered heart attacks or other illnesses requiring Chicago Fire Department ambulance attention. Engine 13 always responded in a timely manner, saving numerous lives in the process.

During a run to the headquarters of the American Soldier's Friends, Engine 13's captain noticed a framed picture of a Dalmatian hanging in the front office. He asked Osborne where she got his "firehouse dog." Osborne explained that she bred Dalmatians for 30 years, and her favorite was the dog in the photograph, named *Champion Swabbie of Oz-Dal*. The captain then asked if she could help the house find a new dog to take over the duties of the ailing Lady. Osborne enthusiastically told the captain that she would hand pick a dog who would best serve the department. In thanks for all the help Engine 13 gave to the charity, Osborne presented a puppy from a recent litter of eight. In memory of the old dog at the house, and in appreciation

Oz looking over a fire hat (1940).

for Osborne's generosity, the firemen named the new recruit, *Oz-Dal Lady of Flame*.

Hook and Ladder 3

Hook and Ladder 3, 158 W. Erie St., was home to several dogs throughout the years. *Nardi* was probably the most famous. A Dalmatian with a splash of mutt and a spot of black fur over his right eye, he was a dog of considerable stature. Nardi resembled the dog of a 1950s television show where kids with names like Spanky or Froggy find themselves getting into trouble with the neighborhood dog down the street. Similarly, the Chicago firefighters of Hook and Ladder 3 were usually into something on account of Nardi. His antics at the scenes of fires were well-known, and upon seeing the dog in action, Hal Bruno wrote that

the water-soaked Dalmatian scampered around the bottom of the fire ladder, smoke streaming past him. Whining and barking, he refused to leave while his human masters, the men of Truck 3, fought the flames overhead. The men knew that their mascot . . . was at his post again. That simple act of faithfulness is symbolic of the part that many fire station mascots play in the lives of their masters

Never one to stray too far from his bed near the truck, Nardi was always first to spring into action. If Nardi wasn't on the truck when it left, he showed his unhappiness by sulking in the station house, howling his disapproval of the men's inconsiderate behavior for leaving without him. Nardi was a hit with the neighborhood kids and, when the alarm rang, he sprinted back to the house to go to the fire. Usually he made the rig. If he missed a call because he was socializing, he hid beneath a table—a self-imposed penance for his inattention to duty.

Each time the men entered a building to investigate a possible fire, Nardi was right behind them, but he always went back to the engine as soon as he caught a whiff of fire. He wasn't exactly what you would call a "smoke-eater."

Nardi freshens up (1955).

Nardi, the prize-winning pooch of Hook and Ladder 3 (1955).

On one occasion, Nardi was the first to enter a burning building. Because of his distaste for smoke, he immediately turned away and started heading down a set of stairs. The firefighters were still in the stairwell, unable to see through the thickness of the black smoke, when Nardi came barreling down, looking for the nearest exit.

Although Nardi would be the first on the truck to a fire, he would also be the first to leave the scene, departing on the first rig headed for home—even if it wasn't Truck 3. Some believed that Nardi couldn't find his original truck, but others speculated that he just wanted to return to the safety of any firehouse. Once there, the firefighters gave him a warm meal, plenty of praise, and spoiled him with affection. But every house eventually called Company 3 for someone to come pick him up. Rather than send a single car, the firemen hauled out the rig and

rode to the station where Nardi was located. They returned with sirens blasting, announcing Nardi's return.

Nardi knew how to climb ladders but often cut his paws when he scaled them. After a fire was extinguished, the men removed shards of glass that were lodged in his paws. Another obstacle for Nardi was the fire escapes. He followed his crew onto the iron grates, whimpering all the way, sustaining bruises to his paws from the uneven surface. Despite the pain and hundreds of warnings, tough old Nardi followed the men wherever they went.

Nardi's fame spread throughout the city when he was entered into the 1955 *Chicago American* fire mascot contest. Nardi received third place in the competition and took home a trophy. When he was slated for a television appearance a week after the contest, retired firefighter Clarence Berger was the man in charge of getting Nardi to the studio for the taping.

Taping of the broadcast took place in the Merchandise Mart. Hook and Ladder 3 was responsible for answering calls to the Mart, so Nardi had a good deal of familiarity with the locale. The 4.2-million-square-foot structure had a curious effect on Nardi's bladder. Whenever the men responded to an alarm there, Nardi responded in kind by answering nature's call in the building. On the day of taping, Nardi did his business while waiting to go on, in the presence of dozens of dogs, bright lights, and rolling cameras. When a studio producer asked for an explanation of Nardi's behavior, Berger grimly responded, "He always does this in this building."

Eventually, Hook and Ladder 3's house began to deteriorate with the progress of time, and they were forced to move locations. Every dog has its day, and Nardi's was on the horizon. The department decided it was time to retire Nardi. When they made the move, Commissioner Robert Quinn paid to move him to a farm in Wisconsin where he lived out the rest of his days. As one fireman described him, he was "one of the greatest mascots of all the firehouse dogs that I ever came into contact with over the years."

Engine 42

In the mid-1970s, the London Fire Brigade came to Chicago for an official visit. The two cities' fire departments convened to share firefighting techniques and strengthen international ties. Following the conclusion of the talks, the Brigade donated a Dalmatian puppy to Commissioner Quinn. *Domino* was a descendent from the Queen's direct line of Dalmatians originally bred to serve the Brigade in the 1700s. The commissioner donated the dog to Engine 42, 55 W. Illinois St., in Chicago's Gold Coast neighborhood, a few blocks from the Magnificent Mile on Michigan Avenue.

Domino didn't ride the rig much—his purpose was better served as a guard dog. During one afternoon in the summer, the battalion chief stopped by the house for a routine visit and was not happy to see the newest firedog sprawled out on the cement apron sunning himself. Upon exiting the house, he ordered the firefighters to keep Domino locked up in the basement, at all times, no matter what.

Later in the week, Commissioner Quinn stopped by to play handball at the house and asked to see Domino. The crew told him he was caged in the basement, on the battalion chief's order. The commissioner instructed the crew to release the hound since "a battalion chief could be

replaced faster than this dog." He would not affront the British by keeping their gift locked in a dingy basement. Domino returned to business as usual, saved from a life of misery in the basement. Anytime the battalion chief came over, Domino could be seen gloating in front of the house, sprawled out a little further on the apron than usual.

After Domino received the executive pardon, he was a natural fit for the role of the department's show dog. When-

Domino in a parade with the men of Engine 42 (1972).

ever there was a parade or official function, Domino was employed to complete the picture. He was frequently used to lead the band or greet VIPs. Perhaps this higher visibility increased Domino's curiosity for an education. At the house, he would take a book from the shelf and, one by one, lick each page out. A barren bookshelf led the firemen to note that he "read" a lot of books while he was at Engine 42.

FROM 1980 UNTIL 1984, *Brandy* literally dominated the firehouse dog scene. The massive Saint Bernard had the good fortune of being able to eat with the firefighters, even if she wasn't invited. At every meal, Brandy sat on the floor, but her head still peered above the table. At the end of the meal, there was one firefighter on "drool duty." His job: to wipe up the puddles of saliva that collected under Brandy's chin while she enviously watched the firefighters devour their meal. For fun, the captain often threw her a scrap from his end of the table, which she would catch with a quick bite. The result was a warm spray of drool soaking the group, while the captain was well out of range.

In addition to her drooling issues, Brandy had a serious skin infection that required a prescription shampoo. The house ran out of the good stuff, so one firefighter accidentally used Joy dishwashing detergent on Brandy. All of Brandy's hair fell out, and instead of a Saint Bernard, they had a 200-pound Chihuahua.

Brandy of Engine 42 (1982).

Unknown firedog riding on Engine 42 (1927).

IN THE LATE 1980s, *Mandy* dwelled within Engine 42's house. Her main duty was giving birth, and she had numerous litters while serving at the station. One litter spawned 13 puppies, cluttering the house with wandering, hyper pooches, known as the "Bakers Dozen." The firefighters had to tiptoe through the dogs to get to the rig. It was standard operating procedure to check under the tires before departing for a call. Luckily, every dog safely made it into the arms of adopting families or other firehouses.

Engine 55

Firedog legend *Bozo* (see Chapter 4, pp. 38–39) had lived at Engine 55 for almost eight years before he began training *George* to run with Hook-and-Ladder 44, which was also housed at 2740 N. Sheffield Ave. George's owner was going to send the Dalmatian puppy to the dog pound because he had been born sick and deaf, but the firemen wanted to try and nurse him back to health and asked if they could keep him. The owner agreed, and it only took the firefighters a few short months to get George up to speed. George was never able to develop his hearing, but his other senses became so acute that he had no trouble adapting to firehouse life.

Hal Bruno reported on this teacher–student relationship in the *Chicago American* on February 23, 1955. He explained how Bozo first showed the new pup that the hook-and-ladder cab was a safe place to sleep. What he didn't tell him was the exciting ride he would get when the firemen ran to the truck. George was doing well until his enthusiasm and overconfidence caused him to try and jump aboard Bozo's engine as it was going out the door. Bruno explained, "Bozo almost chewed his head off, making it clear that George was assigned only to Truck 44."

The master Jedi had to train the young Skywalker not to follow the crew into a burning building because his lack of hearing was a liability to himself and the firefighters. This was difficult for the young Dalmatian to understand because his teacher frequently went into the fires. George wanted to be part of the action and wasn't content to remain outside guarding the apparatus. An angry but understanding battalion chief was overheard to mutter: "I know you're deaf George, but get out of my way." Eventually, George got the picture and became one the city's most ardent protectors of the equipment at the fire scenes.

Lobo served at Engine 55 in the 1990s.

Engine 56

Three different dogs at Engine 56 held the name *Sam* over a span of almost 30 years. The trio was not related, but the crew kept the name because it brought good luck. Because of their successive names, the dogs were, in a way, like kings—each heir receiving the same name of their predecessor with a Roman numeral attached. The house, located at 2214 W. Barry Ave., even has a bench painted in honor of the first Sam. The first two Sams were a pair of mutts who provided their firedog services in the 1970s and 1980s, while the last dog, Sam III, ruled during the 1990s.

Sam the First ruled from 1970 to 1984 and, like any good king, attempted to ensure his royal line with as many offspring as possible. The brown-spotted mutt rode on the back of the rig and jumped off anytime he saw a squirrel; he wasn't afraid to leap off even if the engine was racing to a fire. Sam followed firefighters into blazes, when he could squeeze by them, and was an excellent guardian of both the house and the rig.

Sam's one weakness was firecrackers, and he needed tranquilizers on every Fourth of July. He once ran all the way into a neighbor's basement to escape the noise. The 14-year-old dog eventually went deaf and couldn't jump up on the rig anymore. Sam died when the back wheel ran over him as the rig was backing into the house. The guys thought that maybe he had expired earlier because he physically couldn't get out of the way.

THE SECOND SAM didn't last very long because of his love for chasing cars. A neighbor inevitably hit the dog one

Sam II enduring the winter on top of Engine 56 (1976).

Sam guarding the rig (1970).

afternoon. He felt terrible and came over to the house a few days later with a new three-month-old Labrador puppy. The neighbor said the dog showed up in his yard, but he was too young to be weaned. The guy most likely purchased the pure-bred Lab for the house as a result of his guilt over *Sam II.*

SAM THE THIRD'S temperament was identical to Sam the First's, so much so that the firefighters suspected that maybe his ghost haunted the house. He was known to bring the paper to the crew every morning and always jumped at the opportunity to eat his favorite treat of stale bread. Sam's favorite hobby was chewing on balls, tearing any to shreds—even golf balls.

During the summers, Sam could hear the chimes of the ice cream truck echoing blocks away and always gave chase. When he finally caught up, he patiently waited in line with the kids, gradually moving forward until it was his turn to see the ice cream man. Somehow Sam always managed to swing a free cone and was dutifully there to "rescue" renegade ice creams that hit the sidewalk. Sam acquired a certain joy in being around children, and he protected them as fiercely as he protected his firefighters. When a young girl came out of a house and a local dog charged at her in an aggressive manner, Sam immediately stepped in and stared the dog down.

Sam III's yearbook picture (1988).

Years of following the ice cream man and sleeping on the pavement resulted in a bum knee that required an expensive operation that the firefighters paid for. Shortly following the procedure, hip surgery became necessary. He was put down in the mid-1990s, when all the medical attention couldn't give him a better quality of life. The royal line was extinguished, but long live the kings!

Engine 76

Engine 76 at 1747 N. Pulaski Rd. was home to a pair of *Stormys* during the 1970s and 1980s. Both of the dogs loved to chase rats and were among the most colorful dogs ever to roam a Chicago firehouse. *Stormy I*, a mix of Saint Bernard and German Shepherd, was named after the Blizzard of 1967. He was considered a miracle-orphan of the great storm when he wandered into the house during white-out conditions. The crew took him in, and he remained a part of the house for several years. He even survived the commissioner's order to ban all firedogs. When the firefighters tried to donate him to a family because of the order, he walked for three days, and over 30 miles from the sub-

urb of Des Plaines, back to the firehouse.

Because Stormy loved the cold and preferred sleeping outside, he grew a shaggy coat that firefighters said looked more like a lion's mane than a mutt's fur. (Though his tendency to stay outside also gave Stormy the dirtiest and smelliest coat in the city.) One firefighter reported, "Stormy wandered the neighborhood as he pleased. He generally spent the days sleeping in the alley behind the house regardless of the weather." If a car ventured down the alley, Stormy wouldn't budge no matter how incessant the beeping. The garbage truck was the only vehicle large enough to motivate Stormy into moving. Because of his stubbornness, he was run over by a car and broke his back. Stormy recovered and was thereafter more cautious of the alley.

Stormy made friends with the cooks from all three shifts. He was known for going into the grocery store with them and sitting in the dog food aisle, picking out his favorite brand of kibble for the week. Very well fed, Stormy grew to such a mammoth size that he generally sat and slept anywhere that struck his fancy. When not sleeping in the alley, he wandered into Engine 76's basement where, according to the same firefighter, he "could be heard at all hours of the night leaving the basement and the house. The house had an old metal circular staircase from the basement to the bunk room and when Stormy roamed, the entire staircase shook so everyone heard it."

Stormy also mastered the CTA's bus system. The drivers loved him and drove the pooch on the bus to Squad 5's headquarters from Engine 76. He also used the bus system to travel the neighborhood, his midnight excursions often getting him into trouble. He once excitedly jumped through

Stormy's headstone located at Engine 76.

the screen door of a residential house to engage in a tryst with a female dog. As a result, the house decided to neuter their beloved mascot.

Stormy was extremely self-conscious and never let anyone watch him go to the bathroom. When the firefighters tried to sneak up on him, Stormy either quickly finished or stopped completely. Another peculiarity of Stormy's was his regular attempts to dig up the grave of a former dog buried in the yard. A large rock was placed on top of the grave to keep him from exhuming the body.

During one Easter season, a friend gave a firefighter three baby chickens as a gift. The firefighter left the little chicks at Engine 76 with a relief crew. He thought he had placed them in a safe location, but when the firefighter returned, he discovered that Stormy had located and eaten two of them alive. The third was so scared he was shaking.

Feathers and chick carcasses were all over the yard, and Stormy looked like the proverbial cat that ate the canary.

Like most Chicago firedogs, Stormy accompanied the rig to hundreds of calls. He always rode with his head out the window, and years of this practice resulted in a permanent wind-blown look of droopy eyes and wrinkly skin that made him look more like a Basset Hound than a Shepherd mutt. If it was particularly cold outside, he rode with his back to the wind. When he arrived at the scene, he immediately jumped off and began wandering. The rig usually left without him, knowing that he would return later in the evening, finding his own way to get back.

During his final hours of life, the crew put Stormy on an ambulance backboard and drove him to the hospital where he was put to sleep. The next day, the house had a complete funeral service under the direction of a professional undertaker who was related to one of the firefighters.

STORMY'S NIGHTLY WANDERINGS resulted in *Stormy II*, another Shepherd of considerable girth. Like his father, Stormy II rode the rig to the scene with the crew, but immediately took off upon his arrival. He found other means of getting back to Engine 76, often riding the CTA bus, a trick he undoubtedly learned from his

Stormy II guarding the house (1980).

old man. Stormy II also never let anyone into the house who wasn't wearing a uniform, using the smell of smoke as an indicator of their identity. He died a peaceful death and was buried in the back of the house next to his father.

Duke aboard Engine 76 (1970).

IN THE 1950s, Hal Bruno reported on *Smokey*, a small but tough black mongrel. The house was then located at 3517 W. Cortland St., and Bruno reported that Smokey took "a dim view of strangers touching the pumper." Engine 76 also employed the services of *Duke* during the mid-1970s. Duke's leg was run over by the rig, and he eventually retired to a farm in Indiana. His picture can be found in the 1976 Chicago Fire Department yearbook, but his name appears as the firefighter who took care of him.

Engine 70

In the 1940s, *Mickey* was a black mutt with white markings, and the first firedog Hal Bruno saw riding aboard Engine 70's hosebed atop an Ahrens–Fox pumper. He barked incessantly at the siren as they proceeded to a scene. When Bruno was a 16-year-old fan at Engine 70, the dog frequently curled up on the Fox's front bumper. If an alarm sounded during these peaceful moments, Bruno

explained that:

> [s]uddenly, he'd leap up, make a spectacular midair turn, land running on the floor and scramble to his place on the pumper just as the "man-in-the-box" gave 70 a run. It was spooky how that dog knew an alarm was coming in, until we figured out that his sensitive ears could pick up the loud speaker switch being turned on. Riding that apparatus was the whole point of Mickey's life.

THIRTY YEARS LATER, at the same house at 1545 W. Rosemont Ave., *Beau* ran the neighborhood. In the Chicago Fire Department, a firefighter is considered a "Beau" if he or she has been on the job for a number of years and is more experienced than a rookie. The firefighter is more like an apprentice, but not quite a veteran. Beau was a very frisky Samoyed who easily made friends with dogs and kids alike. Her favorite snack was Slim Jims, a commercially produced beef jerky.

Engine 83

Wino was a "Garbage" Shepherd—a type of mutt with a blend of many different breeds but comprised mostly of German Shepherd. Housed at Engine 83 at 1200 W. Wilson Ave. from 1976 until 1989, Wino was a stray who strolled in from the neighborhood and immediately found her calling. Her breed was so obscure that the men nicknamed her *Heinz* because she was made of "57" different breeds of dog.

True to her name, Wino loved going to the taverns around the house, which at one time numbered 17. She liked to hit happy hour during the week, and the bartenders fed her Slim Jims. When one of the patrons stepped outside for a cigarette or a breath of fresh air, Wino made her exit and proceeded onward to the next bar.

Despite her barhopping, Wino never missed a run, and by the end of her life had made over 25,000 runs. Wino also acted as a gauge for the firefighters, typically entering the fires before the crew even had a chance to unroll their hose. If she ran into a building and immediately came out, the men knew there was no fire inside. But if she ran in and did not come out, the men knew to follow her because a fire was blazing. Because she worked so hard, her routine was akin to that of a firefighter's. Every few days, a fireman took her home for a well-deserved furlough.

During Wino's tenure, a firefighter had the idea to bring in a firehouse duck, a mallard named *Mallory*. It turns out that ducks and dogs do not cohabitate very well, and for about a month, Mallory ate Wino's food and pecked at her with a sharp beak. Wino responded in kind, but the duck quickly flapped its wings and found safety in a different part of the firehouse—she was a stealthy duck. The last straw came when the firefighters decided to bring the duck on a run with them. Aside from the competition that naturally evolved with a duck and a dog vying for the attention of a crew of firefighters, there was the logistical problem of what to do with the dueling duo upon arrival at a scene. The firemen let Wino wander around the fire, but had to give Mallory to a waiting paramedic while the firefighters completed their job. After the run, it was decided that the firehouse wasn't big enough for the two of them, and Mallory had to leave.

Wino died at 13 years old when she drank anti-freeze by mistake. The sweet-smelling green liquid spilled on the ground when the crew was changing it on the engine. Wino licked the remnants and walked to her bed for her eternal slumber. The men and women at Engine 83 loved her dearly and grieved for a considerable amount of time, turning down offers of new puppies. At her memorial service, one of the firefighters brought flowers from a local florist's trash dumpster. While the flowers were slightly wilted, they were a fitting end for the life of a street dog that made good. There is gravestone outside the station that can still be seen today.

A FEW YEARS AFTER Wino's passing, another stray dog walked into the house. Perhaps it was karma or even a

A hard day's work for Wino of Engine 83 (1981).

ghost, but the dog looked exactly like Engine 83's former pet. Upon seeing the new pooch for the first time, one firefighter had a tear in his eyes because "the new dog looked so much like the old one." The crew named the dog *Wino, Jr.*

Like his predecessor, Junior liked to party. But unlike Wino, Junior didn't know where to draw the line. Junior ran with a fast crowd; he drank with the locals at the taverns and loitered with the bums on the street. One of Junior's close friends was a woman in outpatient therapy at a nearby psychiatric hospital. The two passed the days drinking wine and roaming the neighborhood. When Junior was hungry, his friend stole meat from the grocery store and gave it to

Wino's grave outside the firehouse.

him. Junior also imbibed with a group of Native Americans at a local apartment complex. Following the long nights, Junior arose to grab breakfast with the "Jesus People" at a local shelter.

When inebriated, he frequently rode the "L." The firehouse often received calls from unhappy CTA agents asking for someone to retrieve him. Likewise, the area pubs often called the house asking a member of the squad to get their dog that had just passed out. On several other occasions, the firefighters had to pick up the dog from the apartment complex. The downside to Junior's rock-star lifestyle was that he developed serious hangovers. He never

mastered the art of knowing when to say when and, as a result, became very mean the next day. His out-of-control ways were too much for Engine 83, prompting the captain to give him to a sober family.

ANOTHER DOG OF similar leanings was *Schlitz*, a Dachshund who frequently stayed at the house during the 1990s when his owner was on shift. The dog received his name after enjoying part of a Schlitz beer, but at the house, he was also known as the *Sausage Dog*. One afternoon, when his owner had dozed off on the couch with Schlitz in his lap, the crew persuaded Schlitz to get down. The guys gave in to the dog's desire for a beer, and the dog became severely intoxicated. It didn't take much. He was so far gone that he rolled on his back and couldn't get up again. Firefighters described the movement of his legs as a set of four rotating lawn sprinklers. His owner woke up 45 minutes later and yelled at the dog, "I told you that you don't know how to drink, Schlitz!" Apparently the dog had done this before and his owner was not pleased. Schlitz also liked to get under the cook's counter and lick the grease from corned beef that ran off the pan and onto his face.

WHEN ENGINE 83 and Squad 4 were located at 1219 W. Gunnison St. during the 1950s, *Mike* ruled the roost. The Dalmatian had a bit of Pointer in him and acted appropriately for a hunting dog on every alarm. Upon arriving at the scene, as the men got their gear ready, Mike always pointed toward the fire with his front paw. Although it's tough not to spot a fire, the men were nonetheless appreciative and amazed by their dog's efforts. He was born to hunt fires.

After directing the way, Mike followed the men into the burning structures. During "inhalator" cases, the firemen provided oxygen treatments to victims who inhaled too much smoke, and a doctor usually showed up to ensure that the victims were stable. Mike stayed with the apparatus while the firemen worked, but whenever he saw a man carrying a black bag walking toward the fire, he knew it was the doctor coming to aid the victims. Mike jumped off the rig, barked several times to signal the medic's arrival, and then led him to the victim. It was an added bonus for the crew, for the doctor was never delayed.

Engine 59

Occasionally, firefighters are lucky enough to have rare purebreds or exotic breeds in their houses. But one particular North Side firehouse in the Edgewater neighborhood had a completely unconventional line of "dog" in the late 1980s. For several months, *Rudy* fulfilled firedog duties for Engine 59 t 5714 N. Ridge Ave. He was similar to most firedogs in his ability to guard the firehouse floor and his insatiable appetite. Rudy was a purebred Chicago firedog except for one thing—he was a pig.

A firefighter's aunt was a pig enthusiast who collected assorted porcine figurines, and the family bought her a real piglet for her birthday one year. The Potbellied Pig has become an increasingly popular pet in the United States because of its intelligence, training ability, and human bonding tendencies. So buying the aunt a piglet was not unreasonable except that she also cared for two dogs. The piglet's new playmates embraced him as one of their own and assisted in housebreaking the pig. After several months, it was only natural that Rudy acted exactly like a dog. Inevitably, the pig wore out his welcome; the aunt couldn't handle three animals using her condominium as a playpen. Instead of selling the pig, she gave it to her nephew, a Chicago firefighter at Engine 59, and thus Rudy became the first known pig to work a Chicago firehouse. The firefighter convinced the captain that Rudy was a Vietnamese Potbellied Pig that would not grow to be much larger than his current weight. After all, pigs have very compact, dense bodies, especially when compared to dogs or people. A 200-pound pig is much smaller than a 100-pound Saint Bernard or a 180-pound person.

Rudy quickly found himself immersed in a different kind of farm, but he blended right in with the crew. Most pigs enjoy dirt because it keeps them cool in the hot weather. Rudy was no exception. He frequently bathed in the oil pits that collected under the rigs, and his favorite hobby was to root for food on the firehouse lawn. Rudy hated water but giving him a bath was a required part of the house's daily clean-up rounds. Unlike most firedogs, he barked with a resounding squeal during these washings.

Rudy rarely left the house though he occasionally escaped for a change of scenery. Once, the guys at Engine 59 brought Rudy to visit Wino, Jr. at Engine 83. While Rudy made himself comfortable at 83's house, the alcoholic Wino, Jr. wasn't the greatest host. Looking for an appetizer, the pig began to eat from Junior's bowl. Upon seeing the invasion, Junior attacked the pig and managed to get a few nips in before the bigger, slower Rudy turned around and gave Wino, Jr. one hell of a bite. The mutt went running from the kitchen, yelping all the way, and Rudy turned back around and finished the bowl, looking for seconds. The guys at 83 were not too proud of Wino, Jr. that day.

It didn't take long for the captain to figure out that Rudy was definitely not of the petite, Vietnamese variety. Rudy's diet was mostly dog food, but he ate anything— shoelaces were of particular interest. As a joke, shifts liked to feed him sauerkraut for dinner, giving Rudy bad gas for the next crew. When he first arrived, he could easily fit under the engine, but before he left, Rudy could no longer squeeze under the rig to roll around in the oil pits. Rudy had doubled in size during his six-month stay.

According to the North American Potbellied Pig Association, pigs are the fourth smartest animal group on the planet, preceded by humans; apes and chimps; and whales and dolphins. But even this keen intelligence couldn't keep Rudy from an early retirement. The captain tolerated the pig for quite a while until the day the second shift fed him spaghetti. After finishing his pasta, Rudy had a messy tomato sauce face. Before washing up, Rudy checked out the captain's overnight bag and naturally got spaghetti sauce all over his freshly pressed white shirts. The captain had no more patience for Rudy, so he brought him to the zoo at Indian Boundary Park. The captain paid a guy $20 for a required check-up, but Rudy was in great health and was promoted to the Lincoln Park Zoo. He spent the rest of his days at the petting zoo rather than the Oscar Meyer slaughterhouse.

Chapter 5

West Side Firedogs

♨ West Side Firedogs ♨

Engine 18

Engine 18 has housed some great dogs and, because it is the oldest house in the city, has produced many legendary stories. *Sadie* is a rusty-colored, nub-tailed, 12-year-old Rottweiler who currently resides at Engine 18, 1123 W. Roosevelt. She came from a broken home; the divorced couple couldn't find a proper caretaker for the dog, and the firehouse agreed to take her. The years of lying on the concrete of the city's oldest firehouse show on her faded coat. The city is springing for a new building for Engine 18 (the current station's concrete is falling in and can barely support the engine), and Sadie will no doubt accompany her crew in the move.

While her coat may be shaggy and she may need a bath, Sadie is part of the glue that keeps the firehouse together. She is constantly petted by the firefighters of Battalion 18 and perpetually fed food under the table when they gather for dinner every evening. In many ways, she is a surrogate mother to these men and women who respond to the alarms throughout the ABLA housing projects. Despite old age, Sadie is still able to perform one of the greatest pet tricks: a fireman shapes his fist and fingers into a "gun" and points at her yelling, "BANG." Sadie immediately drops to the floor, as though dead, and does not get up until so instructed.

Sadie is also an ardent protector of the house. A fire education truck came up to the building to drop off litera-ture for the house. The engine was out on a run, however. Amidst Sadie's barking, the education division men reported to the radio operator that they "are trying to make entry." The next call was, "we are making progress, talking to the dog." The final call was, "made it into the house."

During Sadie's tenure, the men on the engine were involved in a minor traffic accident a few blocks from the house. The accident required the members to remain at the scene for an extended period of time, and the guys were standing around the rig, waiting to be relieved by the Chicago Police. During this time, the firehouse door accidentally opened. The men of the engine heard a random call on the radio spoken with great urgency, "18, your dog's out." After a firefighter sprinted back to the house, he saw Sadie simply sitting on the driveway of the house, patiently awaiting the engine's return. The neighbors, however, played it safe by walking around Sadie. They even crossed the block to avoid contact with her.

Though the bigger buildings of the ABLA housing projects have been razed, three-story subsidized housing units remain along Racine Avenue. It was during a bitter cold November that Sadie was stolen from the house while the firefighters were away on a call. Upon learning of the dog's disappearance, a fireman donned his heavy coat and proceeded to search the surrounding low-rise projects for Sadie. Seeing the lone fireman, a Chicago police officer stopped and asked what he was doing. After informing the policeman why he was outside in the cold, the cop told the fireman that he had just seen some neighborhood kids playing with the dog. The two men then began an ardent search. Though some time had passed since the officer first saw Sadie with the children, there was a very young boy still on the playground who, when asked, "Kid, where's the dog?" meekly pointed to the second story of an apartment. Sure enough, Sadie was inside waiting to go back home.

Similar incidents have occurred with other dogs in the house. The firefighters acquired a part-Rottweiler, part-Labrador puppy that was once stolen from the yard. A neighborhood kid claimed he knew the dog's location and would reveal the information for $10. The firefighters paid the money and got the dog back. The same thing happened again a few days later, but this time the "ransom" was $300.

Sadie and two friends at Engine 18.

The firemen let the kid keep the dog. A few days later the dog miraculously returned. The food bill was too high.

SADIE'S PREDECESSOR, *HERMAN*, was a long-time resident of the oldest firehouse in the city. He was famous in the Chicago Fire Department for his call to duty when a fire broke out requiring the service of the entire station. A friendly but fierce German Shepherd, Herman was always the faithful guardian of the firehouse when it was vacant. However, this time, in the rush to get out, no one locked the door. A local teenager walked through the unlocked house and started taking the equipment. Little did the youth know that Herman was right behind him. Herman chased the intruder to the top of a vending machine, and the canine watched the boy's every move. Each time the burglar attempted to climb down, Herman would assert his dominance with a firm growl—a not so subtle message for the kid to stay put. Eventually, the men returned to the station, put back their equipment and discovered Herman lying on the ground in front of the vending machine. Looking up, they saw a very scared young teenager who, from the look in his eyes, knew he was in a good deal of trouble.

Instead of calling off Herman, the firemen pulled out a deck of cards and began to play poker, allowing the youth ample time to ponder his fate. The firemen released him with a stern lecture rather than calling the police or his parents. The firefighters knew that the best way to prevent further burglaries was by word of mouth, understanding that Herman's reputation would work its way into the neighborhood.

Herman had an exceptional relationship with the first and third shift members, but the second shift wasn't as crazy about him. (Perhaps because his favorite hobby was staring at the radiator.) One day, the second shift reported that the dog ran away. The firefighters found this a little hard to believe because there was never a problem with the dog leaving. After about two weeks, however, the firefighters assumed that Herman did, in fact, run away. An interesting call came a week later from a woman asking for someone on the second shift. Because the first shift was working, the second shift was not in the house. The woman asked to leave a message, wanting to know if a certain second-shift firefighter could drop off Herman's tags and collar. Needless to say, the dog did not run away, and the woman brought the dog back. The firefighters later determined that because Herman was getting older, they would give her the dog anyway, this time with full approval from the entire house.

THE DUTY OF VIGOROUSLY protecting the house at Engine 18 is a common thread among all the dogs that have stood post there. In the 1950s, there was a pair of dogs who notoriously defended their masters' castle. *Lucky* was the son of *Shu-Shu*, and the two were unstoppable in their endeavors. At the nearby police station, there was a standing order that no officer was to visit Engine 18 without a firefighter. Ignoring the order, two police officers once went into the fire station to drop off an accident report. The company was at a fire, and the two were met by the loud bark of Shu-Shu and the gnarly teeth of Lucky. The firefighters returned to the house to find the two policemen fearfully trying to fend off the dogs.

Lucky was shot and stabbed while trying to stop a robbery. A burglar had broken into the quarters, attempting to steal a television set. When the firefighters returned, they found a wounded Lucky amidst torn portions of the thief's clothing, but the television was still intact. Lucky, living up to his namesake, survived, and was so ardent in his duty that he placed second in Hal Bruno's 1955 firehouse mascot competition.

CHOU HELD THE RECORD for serving the shortest amount of time as a firedog. Chou became car sick all over a firefighter's pick-up truck two blocks before being dropped off at the house. As soon as Chou hit Engine 18's pavement, the rig caught a run, and she was nowhere to be found when they returned—even her dog bowl disappeared.

Engine 67

With their uncanny ability to catch thrown objects, *Rocky* and *Goofy* could have been starring center fielders for the Chicago White Sox. The two dogs, stationed at 4666 W. Fulton in the 1970s, took the game of fetch to a new level. Rocky, named after his preference for stones, chased any rock ever thrown and immediately returned it to the foot of the

Rocky's yearbook photo (1976).

pitcher for another run. Size or location played no part in the German Shepherd's ability to find and retrieve, and he never returned the wrong rock. He particularly enjoyed the taste of fresh asphalt especially if it was the size of a 16-inch Clincher softball. Goofy played fetch as well, but he particularly liked to catch horseshoes in his mouth when the crew was playing the game outside. No wonder he died without any teeth.

Engine 103

The bricks of Engine 103 at 25 S. Laflin St. are soaked in firedog tradition. Homemade crosses adorn the kitchen in memory of fallen dogs from bygone eras. Engine 103 garages the oldest active engine in Chicago, and there's no doubt the rig has spent more time with firedogs than any other in the city.

Lady established herself at the house throughout the 1980s and well into the next decade. The brown Doberman took great pride in riding the engine. In her earlier years though, Lady was known to miss her share of calls and would frequently run after the engine hoping to catch the crew. Unfortunately, she lacked the Greyhound blood needed to match speeds with the rig and usually ran out of breath before giving up. Many times, the police found her looking for the engine and brought her back to the firehouse.

After several of these missed calls, she became a highly conditioned runner. What she lacked in speed, she made up in endurance, frequently making it all the way to the scene of a fire without ever setting a paw on the rig. She used the engine siren as a guide. One of her typical stretches was from the house to the alarm at Randolph and Peoria, roughly six city blocks.

After those long runs, Lady would return to the house parched. But the firefighters never had to worry about her water intake because of the highly advanced, automatic, re-filling water bowl located under the firehouse's leaky water fountain. The leak dripped water from the fountain into Lady's water bowl, and the firefighters attributed Lady's increased stamina to the constant hydration and increased "iron" supplement from the fountain.

Perhaps Lady was a bit too hydrated one afternoon. The cook regularly took Lady to buy groceries, and while he shopped, Lady hung out in the car with the windows open. On one trip, she wasn't feeling too well and when the firefighter returned with the groceries, he found that Lady had suffered a violent attack of explosive diarrhea. The back seat was completely covered in the soupy remnants of "Kibbles and Bits" and the firefighter had to get a new car because he couldn't remove the smell from the upholstery,

Lady and the Engine 103 family (1990).

marking Lady's last run to the store.

Lady lived at the house for over 13 years. One of her last contributions was becoming a surrogate mother to a litter of abandoned kittens. The massive Doberman sheltered the kittens lovingly and protected them as if they were her own. When it was clear that it was Lady's time, none of the firefighters could bear taking her to the veterinarian. The rookie of the house, who wasn't as emotionally tied to Lady, had her put to sleep.

Arson and Lady's memorials in 103's kitchen.

ALSO SERVING WITH Lady in the 1980s was *Arson*, a gifted Golden Retriever who loved every minute of the action. When the alarm rang, Arson dove for the rig and began barking at everyone to get moving. He barked so loudly that it was impossible to hear the address of the call. True to his name, Arson investigated the scenes of every fire, checking out the charred remainders after the firefighters completed their work. He frequently lifted his leg to spray

Arson of Engine 103 (1988).

any remaining hot spots or furniture for later investigations. Arson retired from the job in the early 1990s.

IN 1994, *BONES* replaced Lady and was at the house for only a few months before tragedy struck. The firefighters were getting ready to take the Dalmatian to be neutered because of his wandering eye, and while he was chasing a lady friend at Madison Avenue by the University of Illinois at Chicago (UIC) campus, a van struck him. The driver rushed Bones to the veterinarian where they started an i.v. drip. Bones initially looked as though he was going to make it through the ordeal, but the x-rays told a different story. His hip was broken, and replacement surgery was the only option to save his life. The firefighters needed $1,500 for a procedure to save a dog they only knew for a few months. Apparently Bones made quite an impression, because the firefighters took a vote that night and decided they would pitch in to pay for the operation.

The next day, word of the firefighters' efforts leaked its way to the local news. Frank Mathey from ABC's Channel 7 drove to the firehouse with a camera crew. Mathey interviewed the firefighters about the accident and their decision to move forward with the surgery. The piece ran that night, and within two days, the house was overwhelmed with letters of support and personal contributions for Bones's surgery. Eventually the firefighters raised $2,000 more than they needed.

Regardless of the patient's species, hip replacements are never easy. The veterinarians had to remove the Dalmatian's tail before they could actually start to replace his hip. It took several hours just to complete this first part of the surgery. By this time, however, Bones couldn't hold on any longer. As they were completing work on the second side of the hip, Bones died on the operating table.

Everyone was crushed. It was unfortunate how all the support and love from the city could not change the fate of the poor Dalmatian. The firefighters mourned for days but

Lugnut and a pal outside Engine 103.

wrote notes to all the people who contributed, informing them of what happened. They donated the extra $2,000 to the local animal rescue fund.

SHORTLY AFTER BONES died, the same technicians at the animal hospital explained they had a stray English Labrador Retriever that needed to find a home quickly. The Lab had been there for over a month without anyone claiming him and was scheduled for extermination later in the week. The nurses at the hospital had named the Lab *Lugnut* because of the shape of his enormous head.

When Bones died, the hospital personnel asked if the firefighters of 103 would like to give Lugnut a new home. But before one firefighter could make a decision for the entire house, all the firefighters had to vote on the idea. It wasn't much of a vote because the house decided unanimously that they would care for the new pooch. A few days after Bones's death, Lugnut moved in and remains a solid fixture of firedog strength.

Covered in a plush black coat, Lugnut is emperor of today's Chicago firedog class, setting the standard for the protection of lives and equipment. The colossal Labrador is easily one of Chicago's largest active-duty firedogs. When Lugnut goes shopping with the cook, he doesn't need to lock the doors. Lugnut sits in the passenger's seat with the windows down, leaning against the headrest just like a human being.

Even though he was born on April 1, Lugnut is no fool. Like any newcomer to a firehouse, it took a good month for him to adjust to the surroundings. Because Engine 103 is a single engine house, the firefighters have to chain him up

Lugnut on Engine 103.

cally dragged the desk to which he was tied across the floor in an attempt to eliminate the relief crew. So if Engine 103 catches a fire, change companies park their rig on the apron. The relief crews are so scared of Lugnut that they stay outside or huddle around the old joker stand (the unit at the front of the firehouse that relayed incoming alarms) rather then attempt to enter the kitchen.

His theatrics are well known throughout the house. One day a visiting firefighter was having lunch with the crew, and Lugnut started bumping his giant head into the man's leg. The fireman asked, "What's the matter, Lugnut? What do you want?" But Lugnut continued his pestering, looking for some type of response from the visitor. "He wants you to watch him eat," one of the guys said. The firefighter thought, "Yeah, right, they're trying to pull a prank on me since I'm new to the house." To humor them, the firefighter got up from the table and walked over to Lugnut's dish. Lugnut followed and proceeded to eat, showing off his table manners by efficiently chewing every bite in front of the fireman. Every time the firefighter attempted to go back to the table, Lugnut intercepted him by bumping into the firefighter's leg with his huge head. He also loves to show off his agility by standing completely still on his two hind legs waiting for someone to give him a treat.

But Lugnut doesn't always wait to be observed before eating—his incredible appetite often overcomes the desire for attention. Lugnut will forage for every available calorie no matter what the cost. From crumbs left on somebody's plate to entire sides of beef, there isn't anything he won't try. Lugnut once ate a new fire glove but quickly learned that such things don't digest as well as the sticks of but-

by the kitchen before leaving. Lugnut is usually agreeable and waits without incident for the firefighters to return. But even in this confined state, Lugnut is prone to fits of rage if a stranger approaches, a reaction to his history as an abused puppy who was tied to a wall and beaten. The result is a reliable alarm system without considerable risk of injury to anyone approaching. Only the firefighters of 103 know how to safely unclip him from the wall.

Under normal conditions, with the crew at hand, it is difficult to imagine this magnificent dog being anything but benign. But the protective instinct is strong. On one occasion, a chief dropped in to check on the house while the Engine was out, and Lugnut was described as "crazy" with rage, barking and snarling until the outsider left the building. Another engine company reported that Lugnut physi-

ter he's been known to pilfer. His only finicky exception is coffee: Lugnut will only drink it with cream and sugar.

One afternoon, the men were eating homemade chili for lunch when the emergency bell rang. At the end of the table was also the main entrée for the evening's dinner, a freshly formed, raw meatloaf, secured only by a piece of aluminum foil. After the firefighters departed, Lugnut methodically cleaned every chili bowl before his nose discovered the meaty treasure lying beneath the foil. Lugnut almost finished the entire loaf before Engine 103 backed into the house. The firefighters were surprised to see an overly friendly Lugnut greet them as they got off the rig. They couldn't figure out why Lugnut's tail wagged uncontrollably. After the greeting, Lugnut made a valiant effort to keep the firefighters out of the kitchen by attempting to play ball on the apparatus floor. The diversion lasted for only a few seconds before the cook made his way to the kitchen. It was crystal clear what transpired in their absence. Upon hearing the cook ask in a stern voice, "What'd you do?" Lugnut's ears went down, and he ran for cover under the kitchen table.

After the meatloaf incident, an entire cake disappeared while the house was away on a different run. The firefighters then learned to be more careful, but Lugnut extended his range well beyond a normal four-legged animal. Food should be unreachable on a metal shelf above the stove, seven feet from the floor. Lugnut tested this new boundary, and as luck had it, Engine 103 received a call in the middle of dinner. Thinking they were outsmarting the big-headed Labrador, all the firefighters placed their medium-rare T-bone steaks on this shelf above the hot

stove. Upon their return, they were shocked to find that Lugnut had jumped onto the sink and walked via the counter top to the stove. He carefully placed his lion sized paws between the hot burners of the stove, tiptoeing to the five T-bones before getting busted. The firefighters' latest tactic when the alarm sounds is to throw the food in the fridge and the dinner plates in the oven. Reportedly, Lugnut is working on how to open these two appliances when the kitchen is vacant.

In between meals, Lugnut volunteers as a blood donor at the same animal hospital that housed him for a month. The blood he provides goes to assist severely injured dogs that come through the hospital's emergency room. Lugnut

Lugnut cross-stitch.

has donated multiple times, saving at least two other dogs, possibly more. The hospital staff picks him up in the morning, and Lugnut stays for 24 hours. The nurses adore the dog, giving him excellent care and excessive pampering. He is chauffeured back to the firehouse the following morning, freshly shampooed with a ribbon in his collar. He never seems to mind the required shaving around his neck to take the blood from his artery.

In exchange for Lugnut's services, he receives a very nice healthcare package including yearly check-ups and vaccinations. It's reassuring to the firefighters because even though Lugnut is only five years old, he has already developed mild arthritis from sleeping on the floor. Lugnut receives a thorough exam before each blood donation, and during his last visit, it was noted that his weight shot up to 130 pounds. The veterinarian asked, "What are you guys feeding him? He only weighed eighty pounds when we gave him to you." Lugnut had to be put on a stricter diet after that visit.

IN 1954, HERNANDO reported to 25 S. Laflin St. and made an unusual mark on the firedog community. Truck 39 occupied this house until 1969, and Hernando was probably the only dog in the history of the department to actually make his home in the rig—he rode and slept in Truck 39's tool bed. This small Terrier-mix was not exactly a show dog, but he was one of 12 finalists in the *Chicago American* contest. There was a deeper reason why Hal Bruno wrote about this dog several times during the course of his career.

Firemen were watching television one cold winter evening when Hernando scampered to the door, frantically scratching to get out. A firefighter opened the door, and Hernando ran at full speed across the street to a darkened factory entrance. An unidentified man saw the dog charging at him and ran south on Laflin Street to escape. A barking Hernando immediately pursued him while the firefighters made their way over to the doorway of the factory entrance, finding a 70-year-old man lying unconscious in a pool of blood. An iron pipe was located near his neck, and firefighters guessed the man had been hit over the head and robbed. They immediately gave the man first aid and notified the police. Hernando returned to the house half an hour later, breathless from an unsuccessful chase through the neighborhood. The assailant was never apprehended, but the police and doctors at Cook County Hospital credited Hernando with saving the victim's life—another blow would have undoubtedly killed him. The man made a complete recovery from a fractured skull, and the story about Hernando's act of bravery quickly spread throughout the city.

On March 8, 1955, at the *Chicago American* fire mascot contest at the Shrine Circus, Hernando received two separate awards. The first was the Anti-Cruelty Society's Honor Award for saving the victim's life. The citation was accompanied by a plaque that was read during the ceremony. Hernando was then presented with the American Humane Association's bronze medal for heroism. Hal Bruno wrote, "Hernando was unimpressed by it all. Chasing robbers is strictly a sideline. His main job is to ride Truck 39 and stand next to the chief at a fire. That's when Hernando is happy."

IN 1947, A BROWN and black Fox Terrier wandered into the firehouse during a heavy winter storm, when Engine 103 was located at 1459 W. Harrison St., and never left. *Bum* will forever be known as the matriarch of all Chicago firedogs. No one knows exactly how many litters she birthed, but at least 18 of Bum's pups went on to serve in Chicago firehouses. Her maternal instinct was so strong that the *Chicago Sun-Times* reported that Bum once led firemen to rescue three trapped children.

Bum is also the only firedog to give birth at the scene of a fire. As Bum was moving farther along in her pregnancy, the lieutenant ordered her to be placed on a leash. But Bum refused to relinquish her duties, and when an alarm for 1239 W. Taylor St. came into the house, Bum broke the leash to catch the engine just as it was departing. The firefighters began their work, and Bum's first puppy was born as they were extinguishing the fire with hand pumps. The *Chicago Tribune* covered the Fox Terrier's amazing story.

When the fire was out, the engine rushed back to the firehouse, and two firemen moved mom and pup back into Bum's bed. Five more puppies then appeared. The first was named *Smokey* and filled a previous request from Squad No. 8 for a mascot. The rest of the litter was donated to residents near the firehouse. Because of Bum's unbelievable vigilance, she maintained her perfect record of attending every fire with the crew. *Matches*, a German Shepherd, followed Bum in the 1960s. He died in the line of duty trying to make the rig as it was pulling out of the house to catch a fire. Tragically, his neck was crushed when the garage door closed on top of him.

Engine 77

Blackie had an unorthodox technique for guarding Engine 77's house at 1224 S. Komensky Ave. during the 1960s. Anyone was allowed in, but if you weren't on Blackie's guest list, he wouldn't let you leave. A typical example occurred when a police officer was visiting the house. As he made a move to depart out the front door, Blackie jumped on top of him. The police officer was so well pinned that he couldn't even get his arms free to attempt an escape. Three

Blackie atop the rig (1960).

firefighters had to pull Blackie off the cop who claimed he would have shot the dog during the skirmish if had been able to reach his sidearm. Luckily, Blackie's professional guard skills prevented that from happening.

Engine 66

In the late 1950s, *Bozo* rode the rigs of Engine Com-

Big Red with Engine 66's leftovers (1960).

pany 66 and Squad 7, formerly at 2858 W. Fillmore St. Considered one of the most handsome Dalmatians in the city, Bozo only lived at the house for five years before he disappeared at a fire.

So, in the early 1960s, the firefighters looked for a replacement at the Anti-Cruelty Society and took home an unusually large Irish setter. The *Chicago Tribune* reported the men were initially apprehensive because of the daunting food bill, but one of the firefighters convinced everyone to keep the dog when he said, "After all men, he's an Irish setter," heavily stressing the word "Irish."

BIG RED WAS named for his size and color, not the popular chewing gum made by Wrigley's. The Engine Company reported to fire scenes with quite a flare as the 100-pound firedog's red coat complemented the rig's hue. Several days following Red's arrival, the rig reported to a five-alarm fire at 24th Street and Pulaski Road. The fire quickly grew out of control, and Red defiantly remained steadfast with Squad 7 despite the flames that scorched the rig. From that day forward, Red was always first aboard when the alarm sounded.

Red did, however, miss one fire, which resulted in a blemish on his good name. Both the *Herald American* and *Chicago Tribune* reported a suspicious dinner disappearance after the house caught an alarm. Because Red was sick with an infected ear, the captain pushed the dog away from the truck and told him, "You can't go with us this time, Red." Before the crew departed, the cook had just pulled a dozen pork chops from the refrigerator in preparation for dinner. The alarm was a small blaze and was quickly extinguished. The men drove back to the house looking forward to their belated dinner. When they returned, the only visible chops the firefighters could see in the kitchen were Red's, which he was licking with deep satisfaction. As always, the firemen were suspicious but couldn't prove anything—although the loud burp that emanated from Red's mouth did little to alleviate any doubts.

Engine 26

Domino ruled the roost during the 1990s at Engine 26 located on the West Side, just a stone's throw from the United Center where the Chicago Bulls and Blackhawks play. The house at 10 N. Leavitt St. was in the heart of the Henry Horner public housing projects before they were leveled in the mid-1990s. The neighborhood was the setting for Alex Kotlowitz's *There Are No Children Here*, an account of two boys growing up in "the other America." What was once a ferocious battleground of gang wars is

Domino of Engine 26 (1988).

The Domino Memorial Phone Booth at Engine 26.

undergoing rejuvenation, and the massive public housing structures have slowly been torn down. Domino saw it all, and the Dalmatian's passing in 2001 marked a new beginning.

Domino was a vicious and heavyset protector that challenged anyone coming into her house. When not standing watch in her quarters, she remained a steadfast sentinel in the fenced parking lot, carefully scoping out the paved patch for any signs of mischief. She had a nick in her collar for every scrap she got into, and by the end of her career, the collar was full. Domino also had a peculiar revulsion for the so-called white-shirts, the nickname for the officers directing the daily operations of the house.

The dog began to slow down in the late 1990s, and the firefighters discovered she was suffering from numerous tumors through-out her body. She was put down on February 2, 2001, and in honor of her service, the firefighters painted the house's telephone booth white with black dots. A tiny stuffed Dalmatian stands on top of the booth, and a sign rests overhead, reading: *The Domino Memorial Phone; Sept. 7 1988; R.I.P., Feb 2, 2001.*

Engine 23

Before Engine 23 was at its present location, 1915 S. Damen Ave., it stood at 1702 W. 21st Pl. During the 1950s and 1960s, Hal Bruno reported on two of its canine residents. The first, *Bozo*, was known for getting on the first departing truck. He eventually retired into the arms of an elderly neighborhood woman who found as much joy in the splotchy Dalmatian as his former crew. *Herman*, also a Dalmatian, wandered into Engine 23 on the verge of death in the early 1960s. The firemen spent weeks nursing him back to health, feeding him specially made food and providing around-the-clock care. Herman made a full recovery and lived out the rest of his days at Engine 23.

Engine 14

Alpha is one of the many active firedogs still roaming Engine 14, at 1129 W. Chicago Ave. A firefighter selected the dog from a local pet store. Since his entrance into the firehouse, the once tiny puppy grew into a very large Akita. His growth came from good care and lots of eating. Perhaps too much eating on one summer evening when Alpha was still a puppy. He finished his daily ration of kibble and, after the hefty meal, looked a bit nauseous. Alpha walked around the house for a few moments, finally vomiting into a firefighter's shoe, filling it completely. While the fireman screamed in disgust, the rest of the house was doubled over in laughter, patting Alpha on the head for a job well done.

But what is most charming about this dog is his adventure into the bowels of the city via the underground subway system. On one particular afternoon, a crowd of people entered the open CTA doorway, and for whatever reason, Alpha began to follow them—stealthily hanging behind the pack. The group made their way to the Blue Line stop near Chicago Avenue, and Alpha followed them. He easily slipped past the turnstiles, making his way to the platform without detection. The next train arrived a few minutes later, and Alpha promptly boarded it.

It's said that the key to being street smart is to act like you know what you're doing and look like you know where you're going. Because of his savvy and precision in riding the train, Alpha got off at the next stop and swiftly went up the stairs. However, the CTA guard at this stop sensed something was amiss when she saw the large dog by himself, waddling up the stairs. Alpha was caught. The guard held the dog at her station and, noting the tags that Alpha wore, called Engine 14. The house immediately went to retrieve

Alpha of Engine 14.

him. Alpha was locked in the ticket office, and the firefighter sent in to "rescue" him had to give a description of the dog before the CTA official would release him.

DURING THE 1980s, Engine 14 acquired a German Shepherd and named it *Jane* after then-mayor, Jane Byrne. The mayor was an established dog lover and often went out of her way to help Chicago firehouse dogs. She was known for paying for operations and calling houses to personally extend her sympathies after a dog passed away. Jane (the dog) couldn't adapt to firehouse life, however, and her stay was brief. She wasn't considered to be a "normal" dog as demonstrated by her inclination to play catch with rocks rather than balls.

IN THE 1970s, a Dalmatian, *Snorkel,* was with Engine 14. He went on every single run the house had, regardless of whether it was for the engine or the truck. He was the consummate Casanova—a firedog sex symbol of sorts. He went on runs, but not in an effort to help the men. Every time he got off the truck, he searched for the nearest female.

ENGINE 14 USED TO be at 514 W. Chicago Ave. until it

moved to its present location in 1963. The dogs residing at this house managed to stay away from the limelight that so frequently accompanies a firehouse dog. There was a mutt named *Whitey* during the 1950s that broke his leg during a fire, and a Dalmatian named *Laddie* that did all she could to avoid getting her paws wet, including jumping over fire hydrants and skillfully walking around puddles.

Engine 95

Chicago underwent massive rejuvenation efforts during the so-called "Roaring 2000s." However, the benefits of the booming economy did not reach every corner of the city, and Engine 95 on 4005 W. West End Ave. is located in one of those areas. The neighborhood bore witness to the Chicago race riots of 1968, and today, one can still see remnants of the events that took place there nearly 30 years ago. Engine 95 is a stronghold on the front lines of an urban war and retains bragging rights as the busiest house in the city.

Rather spacious, Engine 95 is located off the main thoroughfare of Washington Boulevard and has tight security with fences and locks on nearly everything. Packs of wild dogs frequently roam the streets, scavenging and marking territories. The neighborhood is akin to the "Wild West," the fierce environment hosting colorful dogs and even more colorful stories.

Before it was at its current location, Engine 95 took residence a few blocks away at 4000 W. Wilcox St. During the 1950s, *Smokey* was a Dalmatian who only rode the rig when the weather suited his taste. If it was rainy or less than 50 degrees, Smokey couldn't be found when the

engine was leaving the house. But if the day was balmy and sunny, he rode the rig with pride. The dog's taste in weather was as discerning as his palate. Bruno commented that if "Smokey isn't satisfied with the firehouse menu for the day, he'll walk across the street and beg for scraps from a neighbor."

Frankie also lived at the Wilcox Ave. address. He was a big brown mutt known for hiding in the bushes. Despite his predilection for hanging out in the shrubbery, his most famous stunt occurred during the Christmas season. The crew attached white spots to his body, positioned fake antlers on his head, and placed a red, rubber ball on his nose. That year, "Frankie the Red-Nosed Reindeer" spread cheer and good will throughout the neighborhood. It's unconfirmed, but he may have even led the way for the rig on a certain snowy night.

DURING THE 1970S, *Madchen*, a German Shepherd, was the first dog to report to the new house at 4005 W. West End Ave. Also at the house was *Sydney*, a mixed Doberman Pinscher who lived at Engine 95 for nine years. But it wasn't until the 1980s that the house saw an explosion of firedogs. The resident canines often overlapped, and at its peak, the house was home to six dogs, three cats, and an opossum. The animals created a symphony of barks and meows, a compilation of altos, tenors, and sopranos. Engine 95 was in constant rehearsal, and residents rarely looked to cause trouble or bother the house. The pets were an effective singing group, and the crescendo of their performance could be heard when the firefighters opened the front and back doors of the house and set all the animals loose. The cats chased the opossum, and the dogs chased the cats, while the crew acted as ringmasters in the circus. The festivities usually lasted for a couple of hours and never failed to keep the firefighters highly entertained.

Zulu, the pride of Engine 95 (1970s).

The "Magnificent Six" included, *Gretta*, *Zulu*, *Frankie*, *Pete*, *Susie*, and *Blackie*. Gretta, a white Pyrenean Mountain Dog, was unquestionably the matriarch of the house. She taught the young puppies how to patrol the apron and guard the station against intruders. The young dogs were always at her side no matter where she went, and they followed her with undying devotion. She had to be put to sleep due to old age.

Where Gretta was the nurturer, Zulu was the brawn. He was born into his role as firehouse dog, literally delivered on the floor of Engine 95. Zulu grew into a gigantic German Shepherd that was particularly hard on the three cats, terrorizing them at all times of the day. He enjoyed working out; his favorite toys were a 12-pound bowling ball and a 25-pound weight. Zulu was a fierce protector of the house, and his diligence caused his untimely end. On one afternoon, a resident who lived across the street taunted Zulu with an inordinate amount of yelling and screaming. The massive beast galloped toward the man, and at the last second, the gentleman pulled out a pistol and shot the dog square between the eyes. When the police asked why he did it, the defendant answered that Zulu had been barking at his girlfriend.

Frankie and Pete were, by all accounts, normal firehouse dogs. Frankie was also known as *Red Dog*, and Pete often jumped into the tower of the hook and ladder as it was departing. The remaining two dogs were, at best, odd. Susie was known for her inclination to hang out with the neighborhood male dogs. She ended up with constant litters, and the crew couldn't afford to keep her or her reputation. Blackie, a Border Collie, particularly hated one of the cats that refused to stop taunting him. After months of chasing, he finally caught it and ripped out its intestines, rolling them out like a fire hose. However, dog karma seemed to be at work when a car hit him a week after the "felinecide."

Shemp playing ball outside Engine 95 (1993).

IN THE 1990S, *Lady*, another German Shepherd, reigned over Engine 95. Her favorite toys included fire hydrant caps and any big rock that could be found. She died of natural causes but left a son named *Shemp*. Unfortunately, Shemp suffered

Skipper in front of Engine 7.

from a condition that resulted in seizures. He could be seen running into walls after the adrenaline rush from the attacks surged through his system. After one of the episodes, Shemp ran away from the house, never to be seen again.

SIMBA WAS NAMED in honor of the main character from Disney's *The Lion King*. In 1999, the Chow Chow was found under the deck of Engine 95's house. A vicious dog, he was a member of one of the roaming packs and probably had minimal human contact. The crew attempted to tame him, dragging him from under the deck and sending him off to a groomer. After his trip to the beautician, Simba still reeked like a skunk, so the firefighters decided to shave him. They left tufts of hair around his neck, paws, and tail, leaving the pooch to look like a miniature lion. When he lay down to eat, he was transformed into the Sphinx from ancient Egypt.

Engine 7

Skipper was the beloved mascot of Engine 7, 4911 W. Belmont Ave., on Chicago's Northwest Side. Because the firehouse is located behind a schoolyard, Skipper knew the bells of the school as well as the different alarms that sounded throughout the station. The Shepherd-mixed mutt went over to the school in the morning, mingled with the children, and when the school bell sounded, trotted back to his post at the station house. In the afternoon, he repeated the process when school was let out.

Skipper was always first on the rig whenever the alarm sounded. Skipper's knowledge of the alarms in the firehouse was so acute, however, that he remained motionless if an alarm sounded for the truck, the other apparatus in the quarters that he never rode. As the curse of old age caught up with Skipper, he couldn't climb on the engine anymore but would chase it down the street hoping the firefighters would slow down.

The Skipper Memorial.

Every rookie in the department is considered a "candidate" until a year passes and they are no longer at the bottom of the totem pole. The same could be said of the firedogs. Skipper became a mentor to *Chief*. Initially, the new Dalmatian was timid about getting onto the rig whenever the engine was called on a run. Chief was frightened by the commotion and cowered in the corner every time the alarm sounded. Skipper soon awoke Chief's instinct by growling at the so-called traditional firehouse dog, forcing him onto the engine. Chief, once afraid of the bumpy ride and loud noise, became an old pro in no time at all.

Skipper passed away in 1993 of old age. There is a monument at the house, displaying Skipper's dog tags, two official Chicago Fire Department identification cards, and proof of cremation. At the base of the monument is a small wooden urn holding Skipper's ashes.

Engine 24

The crew at Engine 24, formerly at 2447 W. Warren Blvd., has always needed tough dogs to guard the house in one of Chicago's more demanding areas. In the 1960s, *Sam* was among the toughest. He was a gigantic Saint Bernard, known for the puddles of drool that collected on the floor whenever he sat for too long in a single spot. He was so large that there wasn't a collar big enough to fit him, and as a result, Sam wore a one-inch thick rope around his neck.

While guarding the house one evening, Sam heard a potential intruder loitering outside. In his zest to scare the person away, Sam shattered a windowpane on the firehouse's front door. The bottom of the window pane was five feet from the floor, and Sam was still able to peer over.

The burglar never made it past the front apron, running like a madman away from the house.

On one occasion, a relief fireman found himself in the kitchen with leftover hamburger meat from lunch. Knowing that no one was supposed to be in the house after the bell sounded, Sam immediately focused his attention on the lone fireman, growling all the while. In an effort to thwart Sam's wrath, the fireman threw a single hamburger across the floor attempting to distract the dog long enough so he could escape. His plan was good in theory but lacked significant bite, as Sam ate the hamburger patty in a single gulp. In the half-second it took Sam to eat the burger, the fireman was hardly able to move closer to the

Sam and his pals (1970s).

door. Trying again, he threw the entire plate of hamburgers in Sam's direction. Sam immediately began to scarf down the meat, and the fireman barely made it out the door before Sam was ready for more.

Sam was involved in an incident at Engine 4, the house located in the midst of Cabrini Green. Engine 4 also owned a Saint Bernard. However, their dog was not as tough as Sam and was often the victim of abuse from the locals—ranging from simple taunting to violent attacks. The men from Engine 4 knew of Sam and knew how similar their dog looked to the mascot of Engine 24. The crew from Engine 4 called the guys at 24, explained the situation and asked if they could borrow Sam for a day. In the early morning, the crew from Engine 4 dropped off their dog, and picked up Sam and brought him to their house. After school, when the kids started taunting the dog they thought was the gentle one, Sam exploded in a torrent of barks, drool, and teeth. No one ever bothered Engine 4's St. Bernard again.

The neighborhood was not an easy place—gangs controlled much of the surroundings, and

Sam guards the house at Engine 24 (1970s).

Sam stood alone with the firehouse. The firemen frequently gave him hefty bones to chew on, and whenever gang members came around the house, the men casually mentioned that the bones Sam enjoyed were actually from the last intruder who attempted to enter the house the previous night. While only joking, the firefighters made their point that this dog and this firehouse were never to be touched. Sadly, the kids later responded by throwing firecrackers and cherry bombs at Sam, causing him to have an unexpected heart attack and die.

Sam held in place for his yearbook photo (1976).

IN THE MID-1950S, *Blacky* was a stray that helped the men fold hoses and place them back on the engine. After Blacky's death, *Rags* came on the job and became a hero. He saved numerous firemen when he sacrificed his own life for the lives of his crew. After going ahead of the men into a fire, he stepped into a puddle of water in which two exposed wires had fallen. Barking loudly before the shock overtook him, Rags alerted the firefighters of the impending danger, and they were able to escape the electric current by carefully walking around it. They had to move on to extinguish the swelling blaze, but then came back to honor their departed brother. Rags's successor was *Lady of*

Flame, a mutt who rode the rig to every fire.

DURING THE EARLY 1970s, a black Labrador gained a reputation as being a vicious guard dog. During a crew relief, the entire shift could not get into the house because of the dog's fervent barking. The crew was forced to place a ladder to the only open window, located on the second floor. They decided the best way to enter was by distracting the Lab with a huge peanut butter sandwich. They threw it to the dog, and he ate it, quickly discovering that his jaws were stuck shut from the peanut butter. During the time it took the dog to open his mouth, he realized they were firefighters and could trust them. Or perhaps he was just grateful to his new friends for the snack.

Schultz II in boots at Engine 44 (1954).

Engine 44

Engine 44 at 3138 W. Lake St. was not directly responsible for protecting the stockyards on the nearby South Side, but the house was frequently the first back-up company to be called if extra help was needed. In the 1940s, the house had 16 firedogs working at one time, but it eventually dwindled to one pooch that became pregnant. The dog gave birth to five puppies in the firehouse on March 8, 1953, but died just after the last puppy was born. The house kept the most charismatic pup from the litter and named him *Otto Schultz* because the firemen felt the department needed more German representation. Otto had a short brown and white coat, floppy ears, four white paws, a white chest, and a cork-screwed tail; he stood a foot tall and weighed 20 pounds. As is common with most firehouse dogs, Otto quickly befriended the cook.

The firemen claimed Otto "jumped like crazy" whenever he heard a fire alarm and learned to ride the rig when he was very young. By the time he was three-and-a-half months old, Schultz had returned safely from 150 alarms. But the 151st on June 18, 1954, was one from which he never returned. Ironically, the fire originated at the old Armour and Co. stockyard building where Dash brand dog food was manufactured. The fire quickly spread to amazing proportions, becoming a 5–11 alarm, and Engine 44 was called in for assistance.

The Armour plant burned to the ground, and the fire resulted in over $500,000 in damage. As the men were busy

Young Firefighter—page 10

Schultz II on top of his food (1954).

trying to contain the roaring blaze, Otto frolicked with other fire companies' mascots and even made the television newsreels. But when Engine Co. 44 finally called it a day, Otto was nowhere to be found.

The firefighters were heartbroken and undertook a campaign to find their lost teammate. The story received high profile press in several different newspapers, and the firehouse cook made daily trips back to the Armour plant, as well the dog pound, the Anti-Cruelty Society, and the Animal Welfare League. After a week of hunting and can-

vassing the neighborhood, there was no trace of Otto, and they called off the search. The firemen never gave up hope that Schultz had taken up with some South Side family, but his fate may never be known.

The Armour Dog Food plant quickly learned of the tale and felt some level of responsibility for the fire company's loss. In an act of good will, Armour's kennel donated a brown and white Dalmatian puppy. Victor Conquest, vice president in charge of research, and H.D. Morris, manager of the general canned food department, made a formal presentation of a Dashmour Kennel dog to the firemen of Engine 44. The hybrid dog was named *Otto Schultz II* by the firemen despite the official pedigree referring to the dog as "Dashmour's Gold Flash." His official American Kennel Club #N–201407 pedigree noted that Schultz was born on April 19, 1954. The Armour Company issued a press release, and the media gobbled up the story. J.R. Holmes, Armour fire protection engineer, and Walter Hage, master of Dashmour Kennels, were also on hand for the presentation. To help Schultz II adjust to his new surroundings, a case of Dash dog food accompanied the pup on his way to his new home at Engine 44.

Answering to the name *Schultz*, the rookie adapted well and lived up to his namesake's reputation, riding the apparatus and even learning to climb ladders. Several months after the fanfare, Schultz was run over by a bus. Good looks and impressive bloodlines do not insulate firehouse dogs.

When Engine 44 moved to its present location at 412 N. Kedzie Ave., dogs became a necessity because of the volatile neighborhood. The house went through over 12 dogs in one year, including one wolf. In the early 1970s, one dog of note was a ferocious Doberman with no teeth. In order to deter burglaries, the firefighters told stories to build up a larger than life reputation for the dog. They usually told people that he got into so many street fights his teeth were no longer sharp or that he bit a kid so they pulled out all his teeth. The Doberman actually had a disease that caused his teeth to fall out, but he was intimidating enough to continue employment at the house.

FOLLOWING THE TOOTHLESS Doberman was *Bandit* of the late 1970s. The mutt was part Eskimo Dog, frequently sleeping in the snow on the apron. In 1986, the *Chicago Sun-Times* reported on an incident involving Bandit, several city dogcatchers, and a slew of upset firefighters. As was his custom, the dog wandered the neighborhood but stayed close to the house. While on one of his excursions, Bandit ran into a couple of dogcatchers—a dog's worst enemy. They cited him for expired tags and promptly put a leash on him. According to the *Sun-Times*, a firefighter "spotted the pet in trouble and shouted to others. Eight to ten firefighters ran to the rescue. About the same time, two fire trucks returned from a call." A shoving match ensued when the dogcatchers attempted to put Bandit into their van while the engines

Bandit jumps for joy at Engine 44 (1974).

were taking their time backing into the house, coincidentally blocking the path of the dogcatchers' vehicle. The dogcatchers became impatient as they were quickly surrounded by some of Chicago's strongest city servants.

Police were called to the scene to break up the squabble. No arrests were made, but in the media battle that followed, one fireman responded, "Bandit is a gentle dog, not vicious at all. Some firefighters take him home with them and let him play with their kids." The dogcatchers alleged that Bandit "also did not have a valid rabies tag or license and was barking at children." At the end of the day, Bandit was taken away, and the crew had to pay a total of $29.50 to spring their beloved mascot: a $15 redemption fee, $2 for housing for a day at the pound, $5 for a new license, and $7.50 for rabies shots.

When Bandit wasn't running from the dogcatchers, he was eating. He became so obese that people often mistook him for being pregnant. One afternoon a CTA bus was cruising by the house. The driver, upon seeing Bandit in front of the house, stopped the bus—with the passengers still inside. She exited the bus, walked over to the crew, and said she wanted one of the puppies when the dog gave birth. The firefighters had to tell bus driver that he wasn't pregnant because he was a "he" who was just fat. After that episode, Bandit went on a diet, but like most diets, it wasn't very successful.

Bandit died in the late 1980s and was replaced by another mutt named *Schatzi*. An enormous Dalmatian named *Sam* succeeded her in 1992. His nicknames included *The Spotted Pig* and *Roscoe*. However, the markings of a cow earned him the name *Holstein*, which was reinforced by his inclination to eat pounds of butter. Sam became famous for eating rancid ribs garnished with fresh maggots that he pulled from a dumpster. He also preferred harder-calorie foods like electrical tape that firefighters had to strategically remove from his rear end. Besides eating, his hobbies included killing rats and any other small rodents; firefighters frequently found old rat bones in their storage closets. He eventually weighed over 90 pounds when they had to put him down in 2001 because of old age.

Engine 114

It's not always a dog's life in Chicago firehouses. With a rigorous daily grind, Chicago firedogs rarely live to their normal life expectancy. There is the occasional exception, and *Tiger* at Engine 114 was true to her name. The German Shepherd lived to be over 15 years old, spending most of her life at the house on 3542 W. Fullerton Ave.

Tiger was witness to the turbulent 1960s and at least half of the 1970s, eventually retiring to Engine #106 at 3401 N. Elston Ave. Living that long is a feat in itself, especially after she had a head-on collision with a car right in front of the house. The guys immediately put her on a stretcher and carried her in a Cadillac ambulance to the local animal hospital. She spent several hours on the operating table, and it was touch-and-go for several days. In spite of all the work performed, the vet didn't charge the firefighters a dime, and

Tiger eventually made a full recovery.

Just before her death, the *Chicago Tribune* briefly covered Tiger's life. The firemen described her as "just a honey of a dog." Her devotion to the house was evident when, as reported by the *Tribune*, "one of the men took her home to a more restful atmosphere, but she cried until he brought

Tiger and the crew of Engine 114 (1960).

her back to the firehouse." Tiger was a pillar of Chicago Fire Department devotion, never leaving her position at the bottom of the fire pole despite the men's attempts to coax her to a more comfortable bed.

Engine 85

In February 1955, a pedigree Dalmatian lived at Engine

85, 3700 W. Huron St. *Bambi* was initially apprehensive about riding the engine, but after a month she ran like a deer to the rig. She quickly became a constant fixture on the engine, addicted to the thrill. Bambi was trained to guard the pumper any time the crew was working a fire, and they actually bought her a coat made out of the same material as the firefighters' jackets for the bitter cold workdays.

FOLLOWING BAMBI, LADY came to Engine 85 in the 1970s. The Shepherd Dog mix was well-trained by the firefighters and always went under the desk on command. After Lady, *Seamus* arrived and often received compliments on his Gaelic firedog name. The white Shepherd Dog thrived on each rat that he killed in the house. He was a gentle dog, but his immense size was often intimidating. Every week, an elderly woman walked by the house and asked the firemen, "Does your dog bite?" The firemen reassured her that Seamus had a heart of gold and couldn't hurt a fly. About a month later, she was walking by the house with two full shopping bags. She approached the apron and said to Seamus, "You look like a pig." The woman was about halfway down the block when Seamus sprinted to her, knocked both the shopping bags out of her hands and left her paralyzed with fear. Amidst broken eggs and flattened bread, Seamus triumphantly sauntered back to his place on the apron.

BULLETS WAS A MUTT who came from the suburban Skokie Police Department in the 1960s. He was in constant need of attention and let anyone enter the house but never allowed the person to leave. He stood by the door,

Seamus with friends (1970s).

gnarled his teeth, and attempted to prevent any guest from leaving. The area around Engine 85 is cruel, and Bullets was shot in the leg one afternoon. The bullet severed the nerve so Bullets had no problem carrying his leg in his mouth back to the firehouse. The guys took him to the vet where the leg was amputated. Neighborhood yahoos also threw gasoline on him and set him on fire. Bullets was rescued by a firefighter, and the culprits were arrested, but Bullets had enough. He left the city for a quiet corn farm in Indiana.

Engine 113

Lulu, short for Luverne, is named after Engine 113's Luverne-manufactured Engine. The Pit Bull-mix puppy looks and acts more like Gizmo from the 1984 movie *Gremlins* than the shiny red and black engine. Her exact lineage is unknown; Lulu was rescued by a firefighter from the alley behind the house.

Regardless of her background, Lulu is the prized mascot of Engine 113, 5212 W. Harrison St. Only fed top-of-the-line Euka-nuba dog chow, Lulu receives the highest quality attention and care. Maybe the firefighters give Lulu the extra consideration because she was rushed to the veterinarian emergency room when she accidentally ate rat poison. Two weeks after the incident, Lulu made a full recovery, and the firefighters ensured that Lulu couldn't reach the rattraps again. Lulu is still adapting to firehouse life, for when the alarm goes off, she heads right to her corner and waits to be leashed to the wall until her friends return.

Lulu and a pal take a break on Engine 113.

OTHER DOGS THAT have spent time with 113 include a German Shepherd named *Leroy* who enjoyed frequenting the local taverns at night. There was also a Doberman in the 1980s who had to leave the house because he refused to do his duty anywhere except in the neighbor's front lawn.

Engine 117

Over the last 20 years, one breed has thrived at Engine 117. Developed first as police dogs during the nineteenth century in the Apolda region of Germany, Doberman Pinschers are known for their exceptional abilities as watchdogs and protectors. The Dobermans of 117 were no different and fostered a legacy as the "junkyard dogs" because of the house's close proximity to several neighborhood scrap facilities.

Setting the standard for future generations, *Brandy* was the last dog to serve at Engine 117's previous location at 816 N. Laramie Ave. and the first to serve at the new 4900 W. Chicago Ave. house in 1981. (Also serving at the old house was a German Shepherd named *Penny* who was run over by an ambulance just before the old house closed. Penny was cremated, and the firefighters spread her ashes into the concrete foundation of the current house at 4900 W. Chicago Ave.) Brandy maintained a reputation as the meanest dog in the city. For the next 11 years, Brandy was king. Known for killing cats that came within a 100 yards of the house, any reasonably intelligent animal, including humans, knew to keep their distance. Most Chicago firedogs are known for protecting their firehouse, but Brandy took this trait to an accelerated level. Under Brandy's watch, only firefighters could enter the kitchen. Even if the dog was restrained, he would create such a ruckus that any visitor left in very short order.

Even some of the resident firefighters had trouble proving their loyalty to Brandy. Brandy had his space in the corner of the recreation area, and a long 30-foot chain kept him in the same general locality. The television was located there, and if Brandy wasn't fond of a particular person or was just feeling protective, it was impossible to change the television channel, as he only

Brandy of Engine 117 (1988).

allowed certain individuals to step into his personal space.

Brandy eventually had to have a tumor removed and did not survive much longer after the procedure. He died in 1992, and today there hangs a mural of Brandy in his old area along with all the leashes that have been worn at the house. (The picture is supposed to be Brandy but is actually a random painting the crew bought and used in his honor.) The next Doberman to follow Brandy was *Ginger*, in 1988. While equally as devoted to her crew, she only lasted six years at the house.

THE DOBERMANS CONTINUE to serve at Engine 117, and *Captain* is always on call to guard the house. Originally a K9 dog for the police department, Captain was asked to resign for unknown reasons. No one else wanted the dog, so the police gave him to the firehouse. Perhaps Brandy's spirit was reborn in Captain, for as soon as a civilian walks into the kitchen, a

Beware of the dog at Engine 117.

fierce growl can be heard from his corner of the room. If the intruder does not leave immediately, Captain shows his teeth and starts barking ferociously. He has his own personal doghouse in the station's parking lot where he frequently patrols at night.

Engine 5

Engine 5 at 324 S. Desplaines St. has seen the temperament of the surrounding area change drastically over the last half century. What was once referred to as skid row has developed into a thriving section of the city. Not far from the house is Chicago's Greektown on Halsted Street, where the rich aroma of delectable food permeates the air and patrons can choose from a number of restaurants. The cornerstone of the area is Old St. Patrick's Catholic Church. The parish used to be a haven for the destitute during the brutal winters, but contemporary times have transformed it into one of the city's most prosperous parishes.

A couple of the dogs from Engine 5 had serious difficulty with their legs. In the 1950s, there was *Tommy*, a Dalmatian born to be a firedog, whose instincts set in after the first ride on the rig. The living quarters were located on the second floor, and wherever the men went, Tommy followed. During one cold morning, the house received a call, and as

The Brandy mural hangs in the firehouse.

Nelli and the crew of Engine 5 (1932).

is customary, the men began to slide down the brass pole. So did the young puppy. He made it about two inches on the pole before landing with a distinct thud. He survived the fall, but it took him a few months to recover from the ordeal.

The firefighters never figured out why his leg didn't break, and Tommy never went down the pole again.

DURING THE MID-1960S, *Buff*, another Dalmatian, suffered a broken leg when he fell off the engine while it was zooming down Desplaines Street. His leg was set in a cast and he was expected to stay off it for a couple of weeks. However, there is much resilience in Chicago firedogs, and Buff could be seen riding the rigs, with his cast sticking out the window. The injury had a greater affect on Buff's psyche than his leg. He suffered a mental block for about a year after the cast was removed. Even after his leg healed, Buff still hobbled along on three legs. Only when a firefighter played fetch with Buff did he run on all fours. Oddly, he came back with the ball walking on three legs.

Buff came from some tough roots. He was abandoned when the firefighters of Engine 5 took him in. He adapted well, but the members of the house suspected that he came from an abusive, alcoholic owner. Whenever there was a visitor who had been drinking, Buff became extremely defensive.

ALSO USING HER keen sense of smell was *Mandy*, a white mutt who ruled the house in the 1980s. Mandy used her extraordinary olfactory sense as a security measure. As long as Mandy was on duty, you had to be wearing your uniform or you would immediately be given the second degree. Firefighters suspected that she smelled the smoke on their uniforms (it remained even after washing) and used that as the basis for her protective instinct. Mandy died of old age; she went missing for several days and was eventually found dead in the basement.

Chicago Fire Academy

Hilly Beans is so small she fits comfortably in the in-box

Buff riding high on Engine 5 (1970).

on Captain Linda Parson's desk at the department's Fire Academy at 1310 S. Clinton St. Every day the captain carries the small white Terrier to work in a travel bag made for petite pooches. Hilly Beans is the smallest firedog in the city, but this mascot is not just an Academy hound. A true firedog, Hilly Beans used to make the rounds with the captain when she worked in various firehouses across the city. The very first time she heard an alarm, Hilly Beans leapt three feet in the air because it was so loud. She adapted to firehouse life, but now prefers a more academic role. When she's not instructing new candidates on proper firefighting procedures, she enjoys chasing squirrels and rats.

Hilly Beans is not the only dog at the Academy. In the lobby, a statue of a Dalmatian puppy sits appropriately in front of an old steam engine. The inscription on the statue's dog tags reads, *Candidate Firefighter Class—Oct. 1, 1997*. As a practical joke at a recent graduation, the brand new fire-fighters put wet newspaper, a bowl of water, and a box of dog biscuits next to the dog.

Dalmatian statue in the Academy.

Engine 6

In the 1950s, Engine 6 was sur-rounded by the historic, bustling marketplace known simply as Maxwell Street, where one could do a full day's shopping within the confines of a three-block radius. The area is undergoing an extensive revitalization, due in large part to the expansion of the University of Illinois at Chicago into the once-tattered neighborhood.

The now-defunct Engine 6 was located at 559 S. Maxwell St. during the 1950s, and *Bobo* was the accomplished firedog on duty. A mean-looking mutt, Bobo probably had more K9 police dog in him than firedog. Every time the engine was called to duty, Bobo ran into the middle of the street and stopped traffic by barking at the cars. After the rig left the house, Bobo stood on the apron and diligently awaited its return. He repeated the ritual for the firefighters when they arrived home, authoritatively barking in the streets to pro-vide ample room for the engine to back into the house.

Bobo had a perpetual reserve of energy, and if he slept, the firemen never knew it. At night, Bobo accompanied a police officer who walked the graveyard beat. He wouldn't return to the firehouse until morning, but if he heard the firehouse alarm ring in the middle of the night, Bobo sprinted back to resume his traffic directing.

Engine 1

Willie, a strikingly handsome Dalmatian, was named after the house's battalion chief and served in the 1970s. The park across the street from the Engine 1 at 419 S. Wells St. was nicknamed "Willard Park" because it was Willie's favorite place to hang out. Though it was an empty lot filled with bottles and brown patches of grass, Willie routinely crossed the street to go there and do his business. He was inevitably hit once by a speeding car, but sustained no serious injuries. Following the accident, he realized he didn't have nine lives and looked in both directions before crossing Wells Street again.

Willie was also a bit of a lady's man. While strolling through Willard Park, the spotted Dalmatian came across a Seeing Eye dog. A blind man had let his dog off the leash to roam the park. The gentleman began calling his dog, but Willie and his new friend were busy exploring the depths of their relationship. The firefighters noticed what was happening and immediately ran over to the park to break up the tryst. The blind man was oblivious to the unfolding events but was thankful for the return of his dog.

On another occasion, the house received a call to respond to a fire. In an effort to restrain Willie, a fireman tied him up to the pop machine, and the guys left on the rig. Shortly thereafter, Willie came running out with the vending machine in tow. The machine had been left on a dolly because the guys were rearranging the furniture, and Willie went several blocks dragging the pop machine in pursuit of the engine.

Willie sometimes accompanied the men to fires. While leaving the scene of a blaze by the Conrad Hilton Hotel, the engineer stopped the rig in order to talk to a police officer who was mounted on a horse. The two men began talking, and the horse put his head into the rig. Willie proceeded to bite the horse's snout, and the larger animal was so spooked that it took off (with the police officer still riding him) and ran for several blocks, abruptly ending the conversation.

Engine 57

Engine 57, 1244 N. Western Ave., was home to *Rufus* during the 1970s, but he acted more like a Southern Hound Dog than an American Kennel Club-registered Dalmatian. He was so small when he arrived at the house that he easily fit in a fire helmet. Donated by a policeman, his claim to fame was a bark that usually started with a low guttural noise in the pit of his stomach and ended with a fury of higher-pitched yelps. He barked at anyone or anything at anytime and was so famous for his myriad vocalizations that the department dispatcher assigned him the number 1262 because he was always heard on the firefighter's radio. Despite this unofficial assignment, he was actually registered with the American Kennel Club as Rufus McGee, birth date, August 8, 1971.

The crew built a tiny bed for Rufus, complete with carpet and wooden panels—a tribute to his pedigreed heritage. Despite such pampering, it wasn't long before Rufus could differentiate between the ambulance and engine alarms. A pillar of firehouse excellence, he always worked and rode the rig on every call. He often followed the men into battle, but that practice ended after he went ahead of the firefighters down a blazing gangway and nearly lost his life in the smoldering ash. Following the harrowing experience, Rufus served in more of an administrative capacity, directing operations with a fierce bark from atop the rig.

Even though Rufus remained safe at the scenes, he could not escape the treachery of the neighborhood. He was stabbed three times (once seriously enough to require 30 stitches), shot twice, and involved in nine automobile accidents—all in six-and-a-half years. He earned the dubious honor of being one of most wounded dogs in the city. The *Chicago Tribune* quoted a firefighter as saying, "Rufus likes children and never hurt anyone. That's why it's hard to

Rufus aboard Engine 57 (1972).

the neighborhood tavern keeper was one of his better friends. Whenever Rufus felt the desire for a snack, he went to the bar down the street from the house. He was always welcome and loved to down the ends of liver sausage that the bartender fed him.

After eight years of service and siring several litters of puppies with other dogs in the neighborhood, the newspapers claimed Rufus died of a heart attack. But the firefighters insist that the cause of death was the second shooting. Regardless, in 1979, he was buried next to the firehouse flagpole, and the neighborhood kids were especially sad.

Rufus sits for a treat (1970).

Engine 68

Though Engine 68 is now located at 5258 W. Grand, two residents made a lasting impact at the 1642 N. Kostner Ave. address during the 1950s. The first was *Brownie* who was rescued from the pound—and a looming demise—and brought to the house. Hal Bruno noted, "[h]e's a great favorite of the neighborhood kids, but snaps a warning when teased. Someone got their arm in the way of his warning, and Brownie got a free trip to the pound."

THE SECOND DOG at the Kostner Avenue house was *Whis-*

understand why people are so cruel and have assaulted him so many times. He's been hurt so many times the vet knows him well by now."

While the neighborhood was less than kind to Rufus,

key, also a mutt, who served during the 1970s. He was discovered by a firefighter in an abandoned building. Whiskey's mother came by the house begging for food every day. The worried firefighter finally followed the dog into the abandoned building and took Whiskey from a litter of 12.

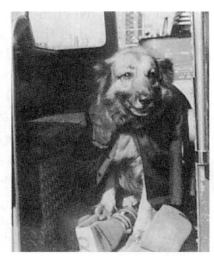

Whiskey ready to put out the fires with Engine 68 (1988).

Whiskey quickly adapted to the firehouse life, learning the shift changes and alarm codes. He loved riding the rig—so much so that the men designed and built a ramp up to the back of the engine so Whiskey could easily climb aboard when they caught a run. As soon as the alarm sounded, Whiskey was off, scampering up his ramp and bounding into the front seat.

During his tenure, Whiskey was also fingered in a pregnancy scandal involving a neighbor's prizewinning, purebred dog. The neighbor suspected Whiskey, so he kidnapped the mutt and held him ransom until the crew agreed to pay for the costs of the litter. The house had a vet come over, take a look at Whiskey, and perform some tests. In the end, the vet determined that Whiskey was sterile.

When he wasn't defending his slandered name, Whiskey prepared his own dinner. Whenever he was hungry, he took a can of dog food off the shelf, carried it in his mouth, and dropped it in front of the cook. Whiskey was hit by a car in the end and buried at the house.

Engine 96

The unofficial motto of Engine 96 is "On the Edge." The credo exists not because of the inherent pressure of firehouse life, but because it is only steps away from the city limits in Chicago's North Lawndale neighborhood. Established by the Chicago Fire Department in 1899, the house on 439 N. Waller Ave. is only one of four active firehouses dating back to the nineteenth century. The sense of unity at the house accompanies this strong sense of history; Engine 96 acts more like a family than a firehouse, and all those who serve or visit are treated like old friends. The house is so accommodating that for several months a pet rooster even made a home there. A canine cemetery lies next to the brick firehouse as a visible tribute to the service and undying devotion of the house's dogs.

Casually glancing at the Dalmatian currently in residence, one would never suspect a name like *Blue*, a compliment to his one exceedingly bright, sky-blue eye. Blue was donated to the house because a family could no longer care for him, and despite the family-oriented engine house, it took a while for him to adapt to his new home. No one heard him bark

Engine 96 logo.

for several months. The crew worked hard to make Blue feel

Blue and Syd of Engine 96.

at home, but it was the neighborhood children who helped him adjust. Blue now relishes any opportunity to play with the kids on the block, who view him as a local celebrity. Many children come by simply to check on the pooch and give him a hug.

His earlier days were filled with making runs, but after six years, he today resigns himself to firehouse duty. He tried fighting fires once but quickly discovered it wasn't for him: Blue sneaked away at the scene, went in the front door of the burning building, and immediately exited on the other side where he stood post waiting for everyone in the backyard. Despite a sole flirtation with fire, firefighters jest that he stayed in the house longer than most.

Like most dogs, Blue appreciates finer cuisine and has a tendency to overindulge when unmonitored. A typical example is the time the guys left a well-prepared roast on the table to answer a call. Though pizza is his all-time favorite, Blue devoured the roast and could not foresee the indigestion that followed. Later that night, after the crew returned and went to bed, he expunged the entire roast all over the landing below the stairs leading to the berthing area. No one noticed until the first firefighter out of bed that morning slipped on Blue's vomit—not exactly the best way to start a new day.

Blue also loves a good chase, especially when it involves city rodents. When asked, "Where's the rat?" Blue launches into a frantic search for the rogue intruder, running to every corner of the house. On one occasion, Blue caught the scoundrel in his mouth and began shaking it. During the skirmish, the rat actually bit him on the mouth, to which Blue responded by quickly squeezing the life out of him. Battle worn, Blue triumphantly proceeded to the apron where he displayed the carcass as an example to others. He was taken to the vet as a precaution, but never contracted rabies. The only visible reminder of the scuffle is a small scar around his mouth.

Engine 96 has been known for rat-executing vigilantes since the house's inception. Blue continues to hunt for rats with a Doberman named *Sydney* who accompanies the cook when he goes to work. Back in the days when Blue was riding the engine, Sydney stayed behind to guard the house. The tandem system worked well, and according to a couple of relief crews, almost too well. One morning, when the change company arrived to stand by, Sydney was in the kitchen. The crew's initial reaction was to leave the house, as everyone knew the reputation of the Doberman. However their position as relief firefighters dictated that they remain in the house until the rigs returned. The substitute crew was so terrified of the dog that they stacked couches against the kitchen doors to prevent Sydney's entrance onto the main floor. Sydney never escaped nor did he show cause for alarm, but even after the engine company returned, the visiting crew refused to restore the furniture to its original location. Eventually, the house furnishings made it back, which was good news for Blue who had to be neutered after he fell in love with a couch one too many times.

Sydney and Blue likely took notes from their predecessor, *Max*. This 1990s vintage mutt caught rats regularly and dropped them at the kitchen door looking for his reward. Max was an outstanding guard dog and inspected anyone on a bike coming near the house. He was famous for his morning runs in pursuit of the *Chicago Sun-Times* truck heading down Lake Street as it delivered papers to the vending machines. Eventually, Max's number came up when a truck gave him a huge scrape that took an inordinate time to heal. Bleeding for several days, a vet eventually was called to cauterize the wound.

Ernie and Janie of Engine 96 (1988).

BLUE AND SYDNEY were not the first dogs to pair up in Engine 96. *Ernie* and *Janie* were like husband and wife in the 1980s, and in keeping with the traditions of the house,

the pair was also known for their ability to catch rats. Ernie, named after a district chief, was primarily a black Labrador, but his distinguishable German Shepherd head made him appear larger than normal. An incredibly strong pooch, Ernie always helped the guys when they returned from a fire by physically grabbing the hose and pulling it to the rig.

Ernie was injured after a pot of scalding water fell on his shoulder. The area on his coat never grew back from the burn, but the firefighters said the mark made him look more like a seasoned member of the crew. Named after Mayor Jane Byrne, Janie couldn't quite match her mate's ability to bed hose. But this German Shepherd took on the role of escort, not always at fires, but for a firefighter's wife who walked to the "L" every morning. After accompanying the woman to the Central Avenue station, Janie hustled back to the house.

DURING THE 1970S, *Lady* was seen as the Queen Mother of Engine 96. Touted as one of the largest German Shepherds in the city, she was originally donated from a K9 police-dog litter and had a full pedigree to her name. She was only there two days before being struck by a car. After a check-up at the vet, she went on to live at the house for 13 more years. She also learned to keep her distance from the rigs after a close call nearly killed her again. The wife of a firefighter, Peggy McNamara, described Lady:

> *Not everyone shared my feelings about the "greatness" of this dog—especially the individuals she wouldn't let into the firehouse, such as service and repairmen of all kinds, firemen she had never seen or not seen enough. I often looked at her and wondered what kind of "magic microchip" lay behind those soft brown eyes enabling her to distinguish the 42 firemen from the rest of the world. She was more than a good watchdog, she was a "dragon slayer" at the big doors, challenging anyone who might enter the domain of the men who rode the trucks. I had the privilege of watching this awesome creature show the tenderness of a new mother when she was only two years old, allowing my two-and-a-half year-old son to caress her in the awkward ways that only a child of that age could expect an animal to tolerate. Ask anyone who knows—she was that way with children. Engine 96, a great firehouse with a lot of history, and a great dog to match—Lady. She doesn't live there anymore. She's retired now, and has a nice marker for her headstone—my family will miss her.*

Lady was such a slayer that she beat up a Doberman and later gave a cat an unforgettable lesson because each got too close to the house. The battalion chief called 20 minutes prior to his visit so he wouldn't have to deal with Lady's interrogation techniques, and the daily short-term firefighters had to put up with similar reviews before settling into the house routine. People walked across the street so they didn't have to tread in front of the house. Lady was even known for pursuing cars if they weren't going by fast enough.

On a hot, summer day in 1979, the large bay doors to the house were left open, and Lady was casually napping on the apron. A local drunk walked into the house, saw Lady, and immediately sprinted away in fear. Lady gave chase and in the fury, the guy jumped onto the roof of a parked car. He fell through the open moon roof window hoping Lady would just go away after realizing she couldn't reach over to grab him. But she refused to stop barking at the auto and drew the attention of the car's owner. The owner found the man with his legs outside of the moon roof and

Lady's final resting place.

subsequently apprehended the gentleman, delivering neighborhood justice accordingly. Lady received an extra biscuit after the owner returned to the house to thank the firefighters for their support.

Lady refused to go into Engine 96 during the 1980 firefighters' strike, preferring winter's icy blast to the warm sanctuary of the firehouse. On several snowy days, all that could be seen of Lady was her long ears and black nose. The strike had some obvious advantages for her; the house had to eat their meals at a card table outside, and because they had nowhere to hide the food when they had a run, she ate it all. Lady weighed 150 pounds when she died; she was buried at the house in the pet graveyard.

Chapter 6

South Side Firedogs

♨ South Side Firedogs ♨

Engine 115

Engine 115, 11940 S. Peoria St., is one of those rare houses blessed with not only one dog, but two. *Hobo* and *T-Shirt* (short for *Teesha*) continue to work as an inseparable pair, acting as the primary security mechanism and stress reliever for the house. Like Tonto to the Lone Ranger, T-Shirt is always there as Hobo's assistant.

A mix of German Shepherd, Doberman, and Pit Bull, Hobo was born in the basement of Engine 115 in 1995. The largest of a litter of seven, he was sired by a previous firedog also working out of Engine 115's quarters. In contrast, T-Shirt was adopted by the firefighters when a family brought the Akita to the house in 1994. The dynamic duo's best attribute is their ability to work with kids. They thrive on entertaining the neighborhood children, and the kids can usually be found playing outside with the dogs after school and all day during the summer months.

Hobo and T-Shirt are also renowned for their ability to

Hobo and Teesha relaxing with the firemen at Engine 115.

work as a joint security team. Like agents from the FBI or Secret Service, no one gets by them without a thorough screening. Spending most of their time outside, the twosome approaches any visitor or car seeking access to the house. The guest must immediately scream for a firefighter before entering the firehouse door. The dogs can immediately sense if the visitor meets the approval of the firefighter. Because of this security, there isn't one chief who can slip past them before their presence is announced to the lieutenant or captain on duty.

If the engine is away on a call, Hobo and T-Shirt attentively stand post on the apron until the rig returns. The house is located in the middle of an empty lot, and when the Engine gets back, Hobo runs the length of the block to ensure that there was no breech in security. The block receives 24-hour surveillance and because of their vigilance, every firefighter feels remarkably safe at night.

The dogs make no bones about who they interrogate.

On one occasion, a rat decided to visit the house. After several intense minutes of chasing it, T-Shirt cornered and grabbed the rat in her mouth. The rodent broke free and was able to limp towards the firehouse door. Hobo took over and went in to finish the job. He took the wounded rat out to the apron where he defiantly killed it as if to make a statement to any rat that might try to make the same unannounced entry in the future. Rodents aren't the only unwelcome animals; T-Shirt will not allow any other dog to set foot on the block. As she has done many times before, T-Shirt will go right for the neck of another dog to defend the house and has never lost a fight.

Kelly finds the hydrant for his yearbook photo.

When taking a break from their guard duties, Hobo and T-Shirt enjoy kicking back with the crew. Hobo's favorite pastime is to fetch large asphalt rocks thrown over the fence of a junkyard across the street. Hobo immediately rushes to the end of the block, works his way through a hole in the fence, and then goes to work on finding the rock. The casual observer would think it impossible for Hobo to find the rock amidst all the junk piles, especially when he can't even see where the rock landed. Just when it seems that the slab of pavement will never return, Hobo emerges from the fence with the huge piece of roadbed in his mouth.

Hobo's favorite sport is basketball and he frequently challenges the guys to games. When teams are made on the house's basketball court, Hobo is always picked first. While not exactly an offensive powerhouse, he can steal the ball from any opponent by pushing it away with his nose and then tackling the ball like a football player chasing a fumble. Hobo is capable of executing this unique maneuver with such speed and intensity that he is considered a serious adversary by all those who play against him.

A FAMILY BROUGHT in Hobo's mother to Engine 115 in 1992. While her name escapes the memory of firefighters, she was a German Shepherd–Doberman mix later impregnated by a Pit Bull. The resulting litter included Hobo. Preceding Hobo's mom was *Kelly*, a German Shepherd born in the house in 1983. Kelly was remembered for his ability to stop traffic when firefighters drove the rig out. He died in 1992 after being run over by the engine when it was backing up into the house. The engineer didn't see Kelly, who was too arthritic to get out of the way in time. In 1993, an unknown Shepherd mix didn't last more than six months after it was run over by a car. The canine was buried in the backyard of the house.

Engine 104

Chicago is well-known for its Irish and German heritage. In the 1950s, *Tim O'Reilly* at Engine 104, 1401 S. Michigan Ave., was a model of this history, representing the lineage of both countries. His roots may have been German, but his name was as Irish as a pint of Guinness. Just after the Great Chicago Fire in 1871, large numbers of Irish and German laborers immigrated to Chicago to build the Illinois and Michigan Canal. Tim O'Reilly was a Dalmatian and actually had a long German name on his official pedigree papers, but the firefighters chose the more Irish name because he was born on St. Patrick's Day. The fact that the house was predominately Irish probably had something to do with it, too.

Engine 116

Salty is a stray mongrel born in the Englewood housing projects that wandered into the house at 5955 S. Ashland Ave. several years ago. She still resides at Engine 116 and was named for the grayish cream color of her coat. Skeptical of her new home, Salty was intimidated at first by the constant action and clamor of life in a Chicago firehouse.

Especially terrified of riding the rig, Salty was never particularly interested in going on runs with her adoptive parents. But soon thereafter, she couldn't get enough of the thrill. Always first on the rig, getting underway for a fire seemed

Tim O'Reilly previewing the World Playhouse movie theater aboard Engine 104 (1950).

to be the highlight of her day. With her hair flailing about in the wind, Salty now stands proudly atop the hose bed during every ride. She also knows the different ring signatures of the squad and engine. If it's a squad call, she barely moves a muscle. If it's a call for the engine, Salty stops whatever she's doing and makes a beeline right for the rig.

Salty was initiated into the smoke-eating firedog fraternity when she charged into a fire at a burning building in the Englewood projects. It was an unusually tough fire, and Salty was forced to beat a hasty retreat from the scene because of the treacherous conditions. Salty suffered from smoke inhalation, but recovered fully soon after the firefighters revived her. She dodged that bullet only to have hip replacement surgery after a car hit her several weeks later. The firefighters spent over $1,000 of their own salaries on Salty's procedure, but because of their generosity, the firefighters still have a trusty companion on their calls.

Engine 122

Duke, *Spike*, and *Pepper* cover almost 30 years of firedog history at Engine 122. Starting in the 1940s, Duke ruled his kingdom at 6858 S.

Spike finding his way through the gear of Engine 122 (1955).

The German Shepherd was an outstanding guard dog, protecting the men in all circumstances. Locals frequently hung out there, and one in particular refused to leave the firefighters alone. The neighbor picked a fight with a firefighter but failed to consider Troubles. The German Shepherd saw the firefighter being threatened and immediately came to his aide in the fight. She eventually was

Troubles has trouble posing for his yearbook photo (1976).

kicked in the brawl and had to withdraw, but her presence was critical in maintaining control of the situation. Troubles went on to live a long life at the house and had to be put down in the mid-1980s. The firefighter who took her to the vet on that final day remembered how long Troubles stared at him because the injection was slow to stop the beating heart—her circulation was extremely poor from old age. She was buried at a firefighter's summer home in Michigan.

Indiana Ave. for a decade before an automobile tragically killed him in the early 1950s. A Fox Terrier named *Spike* was donated to the house as his replacement. Spike grew into his job and answered every call before Pepper relieved him in the late 1950s. After the house received a new pumper, Pepper couldn't overcome the six-foot distance from the ground to the top of the hose bed on the new rig, so the appropriately named Dalmatian was demoted to firehouse guard duty.

In 1975, Engine 122 moved out of the house on Indiana to 101 E. 79th St., and *Troubles* christened the new house.

Engine 126

Several firehouses hug Lake Michigan's shoreline, and within this group, Engine Company 126, 7313 S. Kingston Ave., holds the honor of being the farthest south. In the early 1970s, *Snoopy* was a stray mutt that moseyed into the house looking for romance because the current resident, a Collie–Shepherd mix named *Rosie*, was in heat. Rather than making runs, Rosie preferred to spend her time in the basement hiding from the daily firehouse commotion. The two dogs quickly fell into their roles as a married couple, but while Snoopy was searching for canine companionship, he also found another love as well.

Named after the beagle in Charles Schultz's "Peanuts" comic strip, Snoopy was described by firefighters as a "reincarnated fireman." He took to the engine the very first time he saw the firefighters rush to the rig. From that day forward, Snoopy barked at the sound of every alarm. Snoopy made such a racket that many firefighters couldn't hear the call of the street address coming through the loud speaker. Just as the rig began to roll out of the house, Snoopy quickly leapt onto the engine's rear platform like a conductor jumping on a train as it departs the station.

Even without formal training, Snoopy seemed to anticipate the firemen's every move. As soon as he jumped off Engine 126 and hit the pavement, Snoopy assisted firefighters in unraveling hose lines before they ventured into the blaze. He never missed the initial entry of the hose team, following them regardless of the conditions. An all-weather dog, Snoopy entered every major fire, crawling with the men if necessary. Firemen recall several occasions when Snoopy was covered in sheets of ice after fighting long winter fires, bravery that warranted him the luxury of sleeping with the men in the bunkroom under the beds.

On an early gray morning, Engine 126 was ordered to cover a burning six-flat complex. The house had a brand new firefighter who met his colleagues for the first time as the rig was screaming to the scene. Once they arrived, the hose teams entered the house, and Snoopy provided his standard assistance, escorting the first hose team into the fire. Once inside, smoke quickly overcame daylight, making navigation in the building problematic. There were reports of people still alive inside the burning structure, and fire-

fighters frantically searched the various rooms for bodies. Luckily, everyone escaped safely, but apparently the dog was left behind. The rookie firefighter emerged from the embers with Snoopy in his arms, triumphantly displaying him to the crowd as a victim saved from certain injury.

The firefighter ended his victory tour with a final stop to show the captain of Engine 126 what a valuable asset he already was to the house. As the firefighter approached him with the struggling pooch, the captain said, "That's no rescue, put him down and see what he does." As soon as his paws hit the ground, Snoopy ran as fast as he could back into the burning building. The firefighter was speechless.

But sometimes even the best firefighters need help, and Snoopy occasionally required relief. Firedogs usually enter burning scenes without protective equipment, and this dog was no exception. In two separate but equally intense fires, Snoopy fell victim to smoke inhalation, and firefighters carried him out for fresh air. After a few minutes, Snoopy sprang to his feet only to run back in again.

Rosie and Snoopy lived to a ripe old age— Snoopy had only six teeth

Snoopy's headstone in the backyard of Engine 126.

left before being overcome by tumors. He was buried on the side of the house with one of the largest headstones ever bestowed upon a Chicago firedog. A plaque still hangs in the kitchen with his picture and the following inscription: *In Memory of Snoopy—A Great Firedog For 9 Years of Faithful Service to the Men of Engine Co. 126.* Following Rosie's death, she was buried near her partner's grave.

AFTER SNOOPY, a Shepherd mix named *Stuka* commanded the house throughout the 1980s until he was stolen and thrown into a ring with two Pit Bulls. His tragic death paved the way for today's *Smokey*. The Shepherd has a strong Akita bloodline giving him a larger than average size and one bright blue eye. In and out of the firehouse, Smokey is most appreciated for talents as an alert guard dog that have led to the prevention of several burglaries.

Smokey is also wary of any new faces to the firehouse, especially those without a department uniform. One such example was when an ambulance change shift came over

Stuka of Engine 126 (1988).

to the vacant house to stand by for Engine 126's original ambulance crew. Smokey reluctantly allowed the relief crew into the house but absolutely refused to let them near the kitchen. When the crew arrived from their run, they found the personnel cornered in the front of the house,

eagerly waiting to be relieved.

When he's not protecting the house, Smokey's looking for his next meal. He prefers just about any kind of meat, but corned beef is undoubtedly his favorite. Just as firefighters were sitting down for a good Irish meal one day, they got a run. They were in such a rush that they forgot to secure the food and shortly after their departure, Smokey went to each individual plate and ate only the corned beef, leaving everything else untouched.

The dog frequently left the firehouse at random times only to return later the next morning. On one of his sojourns, Smokey rolled around with a dead fish lying along the Lake Michigan beach. Despite several washings, he still smelled like ripe fish oil. One of the firefighters eventually took Smokey home. Smokey no longer wanders because of the increased exercise he receives at the firefighter's home. He has led a two-hour chase for a deer and always gives a rabbit a run for his money. Smokey now lives a semi-retired life, only coming into the firehouse occasionally with his owner.

Engine 19

While Truck 11 from Engine 19's house at 3421 S. Calumet Ave. was getting fuel for their rig in the early 1980s, the firefighters found *Bruno* at the gas station. He was milling about on the pump island, and the station attendant didn't want the vagrant dog around because it was bad for business. The firefighters asked the captain if they could adopt the part Shepherd, part Collie and received a unanimous vote of support from the rest of the house. The 110-pound pooch became an instant fixture at the house.

Bruno found his calling as soon as he heard the first bell ring. He immediately jumped onto the rig and was ready to go. Subsequently, he made almost every call during his time at Engine 19, and without suffering any bruises or broken bones. Not only was he extremely safety-conscious, the firefighters said that Bruno actually made their "push-out" time better because he would frequently wake the guys up at night and bark until the rig started moving out of the house.

Bruno often slept with the guys on their bunks. They appreciated his service and steadfast loyalty so much that they made room for the huge beast rather than try to kick him out. During one fire at 36th and Giles, the firemen went to the roof of a building to punch holes in it for ventilation. While working, they heard the familiar jingle of Bruno's collar. When they turned around, they saw Bruno tentatively coming toward them. He had climbed the main ladder onto the roof to be with the guys. This feat was remarkable because dogs are often afraid of climbing open steps, let alone a two-story house. The men had to carry the hefty dog back down because he couldn't reverse his climb. Bruno eventually died of cancer contracted from the smoke he had inhaled while working at fires.

Smokey from Engine 126 taking a break from the day's routine.

AFTER BRUNO, *SPANNER* was a part of the house during the 1990s. The Dalmatian was thick-boned and able to jump and snap a treat from a six-foot firefighter with a vertically raised arm.

Engine 2

During the 1950s, a Dalmatian was a member of Squad 8 at the Engine 2 house formerly located at 2421 S. Lowe Ave. in Chinatown. *Yick* was named after a scholarly 80-year-old Chinese man who occasionally dropped by the house to philosophize with the men.

Yick was a finalist in Hal Bruno's mascot competition and was known for his undying devotion to the defense of the engine. Firefighters, police officers, and other city workers knew to stay far away from Squad 8 when the men were at a fire. If Yick didn't recognize the person approaching the rig, he bit them without reservation or provocation. Hal Bruno reported that during an extra-alarm fire, a hose ruptured, and the deputy chief ordered a firefighter to get a clamp for the tattered line. The fireman made the mistake of trying to get the clamp from Squad 8 and complained that Yick "tries to bite me when I touch the rig." The captain responded dryly, "Bite him back, but get the hose clamp!"

into one of Chicago's first mascot competitions. On September 5 and 6, 1937, the contest to find the best firedog in the city was held at the first annual Firefighter's Chicago Charter Jubilee. Bruno was one of ten dogs judged at the event.

Engine 52

During the 1950s, a young boy brought a three-week-old dog into the house formerly at 4710 S. Elizabeth St. The combination Airedale and Dachshund was simply called *Brown* and remained with Engine 52 for over 15 years. He was a natural, and the tiny pooch made every run, dexterously scurrying up the running board to the engineer's seat and then to the top of the hose bed where he proudly rode his chariot.

In his younger days, Brown followed the men into the blazes, and according to Hal Bruno, "[w]hen the fire was out, or became too widespread for the men to remain inside, Brown would stand at the rear of the engine. Not until each man was accounted for would Brown resume his place on the front seat." Brown was a friend to the neighborhood too, and local children could easily approach him, playfully wrestle, pull his ears, or sit quietly and pet him. The reddish mutt loved the attention but knew when it was time to protect his turf. Brown once took down a Doberman Pinscher, and although he took some serious blows (his ripped stomach needed several stitches), he sent the menacing Doberman limping back to the junkyard.

Brown slowed down a bit in his golden years, but his enthusiasm for being a firedog never waned. He developed arthritis in his hips and had to take numerous pills several times a day. Later, he lost many of his teeth when he devel-

The crew of Engine 2 praising Yick for a job well done (1950).

FOLLOWING YICK'S DEATH, Squad 8 requested a puppy from *Bum* of Engine 103 who was expecting a new litter. Baptized in fire, *Smokey* was the only firedog to be born at the scene of a call. The firefighters were extinguishing the blaze with hand pumps as Smokey was being born. When the fire was out, the engine rushed back to the firehouse, and two firemen moved Bum to her bed. Five more puppies were born. The first, Smokey, filled the request from Squad 8 for a mascot. The rest of the litter was donated to residents near the firehouse.

THOUGH THE HOUSE has since been destroyed, the memories of *Dottie* and *Bruno* still haunt the lot. Dottie preceded Bruno in the 1930s, but the latter dog was entered

Brown aboard Engine 52 (1960).

oped cancer. Though Brown no longer went into burning buildings with these ailments, he still made the rig on nearly every call. When the city bought new trucks, Brown had difficulty getting aboard because the new enclosed cabs were too high for him to jump into. He never gave up trying, and the men, recognizing his continued desire to go to the scene, hoisted him onto his perch in the front seat. On the return trip home, he still counted each of the firemen, making sure that every crewmember was safe and accounted for. Fifteen years after he arrived, Brown died in the place he loved.

Engine 61

Born in 2000, *Ashes* is the dog currently occupying Engine 61 on Chicago's South Side at 5349 S. Wabash Ave. The firefighters rescued the German Shepherd from a

gang of marauding kids and took her home. Ashes didn't immediately adapt to firehouse life. It took her some time to go on a run with the firefighters, and the constant alarms spooked her. She was able to make her first run within a couple of months of being at the house however. Ashes still has trouble at the scene of a fire, preferring to sit in the engineer's seat and wait until the action is over. Her abused past might be the cause of her timid approach to all the frantic sirens, people, and smells. Relieved when she sees her crew streaming out of a blaze, Ashes particularly enjoys the attention she receives when the firefighters begin cleaning up the wreckage from a fire.

Her favorite pastime is chasing rats in the parking lot behind the house, but she doesn't catch them for food. Ashes prefers dog food and Frosty Paws, a frozen ice cream concoction specially made for dogs. When the crew isn't looking, she'll even wolf down an entire stick of butter on occasion. She also enjoys sitting on the chairs located in the gazebo behind the house. Whenever the firefighters are lounging outside, Ashes joins them and sits on a chair, looking like she has something to say. The firefighters are waiting for the day when she decides to join their lively conversations.

Ashes is free to roam throughout the house and front yard, but this privilege only came because of the lessons taught by a veteran firedog. Over the summer of 2001, Engine 61's apparatus floor and apron were being replaced. As a result, the crew was housed at the Engine 60 quarters for over a month while the new concrete was poured. Engine 60's dog, an old-timer named *Smokey*, didn't quite take to the active puppy when they first met.

While at Engine 61, Ashes was kept on a long chain that

Ashes of Engine 61.

IN THE MID-1960S, *Brownie*, a mutt named for the color of his fur, accompanied the men on every call. One afternoon, the firefighters responded to a fire in a chic high-rise apartment complex. After the danger had passed, they were putting the hose lines back on the engine, and the captain was talking with a couple of residents. Brownie was gallivanting outside while the men were working, when he suddenly zoomed into the fashionable lobby, pooped on the plush carpet, and walked back out the door as if nothing had ever happened. It was never confirmed who cleaned up Brownie's "brownie," but no firefighter ever owned up to it.

IN 1954, ENGINE 61 and Squad 3 had the busiest house in Chicago, answering 4,546 calls. A gangly mutt named

allowed her to sit in front of the house along 55th Street. Ashes escaped from her chain one morning and sauntered to the middle of 55th Street. Smokey, recognizing that Ashes could get herself killed, sat on the curb and barked until Ashes came back onto the grass in front of the house.

As long as the two were roommates, Smokey kept his job of keeping Ashes in line. Whenever Ashes drifted somewhere she wasn't supposed to go, Smokey, quite the parent, barked until she stopped and came back to the house. By the time Engine 61's floor was repaired, Ashes was fully trained in the acceptable protocols and basic survival skills of the firehouse. To this day, the firefighters say that after Ashes moved back to her old house at Engine 61, she listened more attentively to the firefighters and became more obedient.

Ashes posing with the men of Engine 61.

Muggs found her way to the house after the firemen responded to an inhalator call. She belonged to the victim, Robert Herman, who had just been revived. The landlord of the building exclaimed, "Either the dog goes or Bobby goes." So, the firemen took Muggs back to the house. From that day forward, Muggs became a firedog through and through. The rig answered an average of 12 or more calls a day, and Muggs made every one, sitting next to the engineer in the front seat.

Muggs was one of 12 finalists in Hal Bruno's *Chicago American* mascot competition, entered not only for her diligence in responding to every call, but also for her duties as a firehouse mother. She delivered five puppies in the basement of the house. Having the puppies didn't sway her passion for riding, for she was back in action only two weeks after her maternity leave.

IN THE LATE 1920s, the house had a dog named *Chance*, whose leg was run over by the rig as it was pulling out of the station. At the time, an ADT security agent was at the house installing new equipment. In those days, ADT personnel were allowed to carry a sidearm, and the captain asked the man if he could put the dog out of his misery. Agreeing, the security agent cruelly threw the small pooch into the air and proceeded to shoot it as it came back down. The dog died before he hit the floor, and the agent was no longer welcome in the firehouse.

Engine 62

Engine 62, 34 E. 114th St., sits in a quaint residential area between the Roseland and West Pullman neighborhoods on the far South Side of Chicago. Their firedogs were so friendly that even the mail carrier liked them: In an unlikely coup, two dogs traded their Chicago Fire Department careers for a new one with the U.S. Postal Service. While these dogs may have been unfaithful to the fire department, at least they continued their undying devotion in civil service.

The first turncoat was *Deputy Dog*, also simply known as the *Deputy*, a Bloodhound with strong German Shepherd attributes. In the early 1980s, Deputy Dog began to show his true colors. While he apparently enjoyed firehouse life, the Deputy would anxiously await the arrival of the mailman so he could help deliver the mail to the block. Initially the mailman was skeptical of his new friend (what carrier wouldn't be?), but after time, he began to appreciate the Deputy's service as guardian and assistant. This continued for several weeks until the Deputy's travels stretched beyond the block of the firehouse. Eventually he was making the entire run with the mailman before returning to the firefighters for dinner. After several weeks, the firefighters couldn't hold Deputy Dog back any longer and gave him to the mailman so the happy pooch could finish his career with the post office.

AFTER THE DEPUTY left the firehouse in the late 1980s, they brought in *Mutley*, a Husky–German Shepherd mix. Maybe it was the fact that Mutley was replacing the Deputy at the firehouse, or that they both had German Shepherd blood, but as soon as the *Deputy* finished his days as a postal pooch, Mutley took an immediate liking to the mailman as well. Mutley began going on mail runs as soon as the Deputy passed away. This mailman knew the value of a good firedog—their unwavering sense of protection is something you can't find in a pet store. It was only a matter of time before the carrier ended up keeping this dog as well. Perhaps the dogs actually preferred federal service over city employment, or maybe the mailman just had the golden touch.

FIREFIGHTERS ADAMANTLY CLAIM that *Otis* will not be making any mail runs in the near future. Engine 62's current mutt seems to be enjoying firehouse life much more than his

Otis guarding Engine 62's rig.

previous job as a local security guard, which is only a fancy way of saying he came from a junkyard. While he comes from some pretty rough roots, he is scared to death of thunder and lightening.

Otis demonstrating his jumping skills.

Firefighters claim Otis is just a big house cat with cat-like jumping abilities. It was a blistering, hot summer day when Engine 62 caught a run and put Otis outside in the parking lot until they returned. Instead of guarding the cars, the firefighters found Otis lying on the cool firehouse floor with the air conditioner. While they were gone, Otis had jumped onto his doghouse in the car lot and pushed the window air conditioner into the firehouse with his paws. When the air conditioner hit the floor, he climbed into the open window, and jumped to the floor. Amazingly, the air conditioner never stopped running.

Another day, Otis was caught outside during a heavy rainstorm and absolutely had to escape the thunder and lightning. The guys were in the kitchen, and one of the crew happened to see Otis jumping up so high that his paw was hitting the window, six feet above the door. The firefighters ended his misery and quickly brought him inside.

Engine 84

From its medieval castle-like design to the unique fireplace that warms the crew during the winter months, the Engine 84 firehouse, 6204 S. Green St., looks like no other in the city. Like any stronghold in a conflicted area, the house has seen its share of ardent protectors. At least six dogs have served in this fortress, while an additional four dogs were at Engine 84's previous house at 5721 S. Halsted St.

Muggs initially rode with Truck 51 until Engine 84 moved into the house on Green Street. The Shepherd-mix left a legacy as one of the most ferocious guard dogs ever to serve in a Chicago firehouse. Muggs was known for traversing the house like a military patrolman on watch, only allowing the most familiar firefighters past his imaginary border. During the riotous 1960s, two policemen almost drew their weapons on him after they were pinned against the wall of an empty firehouse. Luckily the firefighters got back in time to call him off.

One morning, a relief crew was sent over to Engine 84 to cover for the firefighters who already departed to answer a call. The change shift radioed the battalion chief who was at the scene, "Relief to Engine 84, we're on the air at the apron." The battalion chief responded, "What's a matter, Muggs won't let you in?" They responded, "The city doesn't pay us enough to be lion tamers." The relief team never got within ten feet of the garage door to pull in their rig.

Muggs was ruthless on the rookies. It was considered a good day if a new firefighter could get into the house without getting yelled at or physically accosted. Muggs never tol-

erated any of their freshman antics and was known to turn on any tenderfoot who wasn't pulling his weight. He was described by one firefighter as "a real back-stabbing junkyard dog." If you were lucky enough to be able to pet him for several minutes and didn't do an adequate job, Muggs let you know with a fierce bark or even a quick nip to drive home the point.

Muggs also followed the "one on, two off" schedule that Chicago firefighters regularly work. He'd put in his full 24-hour day at the house and just as the next day's crew came in to relieve the off-going shift, Muggs took two days off in the neighborhood before returning home. He even went so far as to take "furlough," a scheduled vacation, like all the other firefighters. Muggs routinely left for a week at a time until the house got a call from a remote location in the city asking the firefighters to come and pick up their dog.

A group of teenagers used to pass by to taunt Muggs after school. The teens knew exactly the length of his chain and how far out it ran onto the apron. They went up to within several inches of Muggs's snarling snout to show him that they weren't intimidated by his act. This continued

Muggs's headstone

for a couple of weeks, and Muggs was limited to giving them the best verbal abuse he could dish out. One afternoon, the firefighters let out another two feet of chain on his leash, and when the kids came by to taunt him, Muggs gave them a scare they never forgot. Muggs was left satisfied, and the teens never pushed his buttons again.

After 13 years of service, Muggs died when he was run over by a truck. An obituary ran in the newspaper, and the firefighters buried him in front of the house. The violet cross-shaped slab of granite stands on the corner with "MUGGS" spelled out vertically and the dates of his life (07/01/65–04/07/78) on the arms of the cross.

THE WEEK FOLLOWING Muggs's death, *Sam* a German Shepherd, moved in and lived with the house until 1987 when he died of natural causes. The chocolate Labrador named *Rambo* lived in 84's quarters with Sam for only a few months before he was taken to the veterinarian for an infection. Rambo had an allergic reaction to the prescribed penicillin and died the same day.

IN THE LATE 1980S, *Jake* was a junkyard mutt that was donated to the house after Sam died. Jake had a hyper temperament and frequently jumped out of windows five feet from the ground. Jake also got a kick anytime the guys left for a call—for some reason the flashing lights on the engine had a mesmerizing affect on him. If allowed, Jake stared at the lights endlessly; one time he became so hypnotized by them that he tried to bite the light beam and knocked himself out on the wall instead.

The Rambo painting stands proudly in Engine 84's house.

FOLLOWING JAKE'S DEATH in the late 1980s, a knight named *Shep* moved into this firefighting fortress. Shep was a large, seasoned German Shepherd with an extremely deep bark. Visitors were cautioned with a Beware of Dog sign on the door, and Shep backed up the warning as soon as their presence was known. His favorite hangout was in front of the house's fireplace. Shep died in May, 2002, and was buried in the back of the house. *Shredder* arrived in 2000 and was Shep's sidekick before he died. True to his name, the Rottweiler will destroy anything if given the opportunity.

AT ENGINE 84'S previous Halsted Street location, the earliest canine tenant was probably *Fanny*, a mutt, in the 1920s. Then *Satan* created quite a stir in 1960s; the Doberman was described as "a

Shep attempts to drive Truck 51 (1997).

Shredder enjoying the autumn sun in front of Engine 84.

mean son of a bitch." The house went from the hell to heaven with *King* in the 1970s. An exemplary watchdog, King prevented the neighbors from stealing the television and the firefighters' personal belongings. The German Shepherd had an easygoing personality and was known for such circus tricks as eating small, lit firecrackers. He was also remembered for his ability to terrify strangers and push up flowerbeds. His running mate was *Daisy*, a Toy Collie that the house received as a puppy.

One warm day the front doors were open, and the members were lounging outside when an unknown man walked up to the house and started telling the firefighters how much he admired King. The guy said he was a pro and could steal any dog, but he'd never dare trying to take a firehouse dog. One of the firefighters joked, "Go ahead, try it." Seconds later, the bell rang and the rig departed in a cloud of exhaust from the old Mack. They returned, and King was nowhere to be found. They never saw him again.

Engine 101

The black Labrador at Engine 101, at 2240 W. 69th St., has a different name—*Irene*, *Pepper*, or *Pee-Dog*—depending on the shift. Donated to the house in 1990 by a neighbor who claimed that she was a menacing mutt who tore up the yard, ate the grass, and trampled flowers, Irene had a difficult time adapting to the firehouse lifestyle. She was thin, scraggly, and sensitive to any loud noise or sudden movements. The truth is that the neighbor beat her ruthlessly, and Irene's timid ways were a result of an abusive upbringing. Whenever confronted with a taxing situation, Irene urinated on the spot and the guys at the house usually had to follow her with a mop to clean up after her accidents. As a result, she acquired the nickname of *Pee-Dog*.

After a round of needed shots, daily feedings, and old-fashioned TLC, Irene gradually adapted and trusted the members of the house. Three months later, the firefighters were amazed when the previous owner returned to ask for Pepper back. Reluctantly, the crew brought Irene to the previous owner's house. When she saw the owner again, Irene immediately attacked him because she remembered the way he used to beat her. The owner was happy to emerge alive from the incident and told the crew they "could keep the deranged mutt." She was with them for over 12 years and became a valuable asset to the house, complete with authentic Chicago Fire Department identification.

After Irene retired from riding the rigs, she helped the crew in other ways. She knew the individual signals that echo through the house. If the alarm rang twice, she didn't move because she knew it was for the ambulance. If it rang three or four times, she made her way over to the

Irene of Engine 101.

apron after the rigs left to guard the house until they returned. Irene's commitment was unwavering, and the firefighters often came back to find her covered in snow. Because of her years of devotion, she developed hip problems from lying on the apron.

Irene was incredibly friendly, outgoing, good with kids, and playful (she liked "bite the chief," tug-of-war, and fetch); like any dog, she enjoyed having her belly rubbed. She faithfully greeted the new shift of firefighters when they arrived in the morning. An irate citizen once stabbed her, but aside from that horrific act, the neighborhood championed her. She wouldn't eat ground beef but enjoyed her daily ration of dog biscuits.

When she saw Engine 101 heading for home, Irene jumped into the street and stayed there until the engine was fully backed into the house. This practice twice resulted in being hit by a car. Experience taught her to be a bit more careful and look both ways before venturing out into the street, but tragically she was hit a third time in May, 2002, and did not recover from her injuries.

THE 1980S BROUGHT *Babe*, a mammoth German Shepherd. Despite her unruly looks, Babe was a meek, well-tempered firehouse dog. Most dogs don't like fireworks because they affect their highly sensitive hearing, and they usually react with violent barking or painful whimpering. One Fourth of July, Babe responded to the fireworks by attempting to run away from the source of the noise, eventually escaping the confines of the house and ending up at Midway Airport. Many Chicago firedogs can brag about dodging cars, but no other dog has ever laid claim to playing chicken with commercial jetliners. Babe roamed the jetways and tarmacs for over an hour before the pilot of a taxiing plane reported her to ground control. The control tower gave clearance to airport security to attempt recovery of Babe on the active runway.

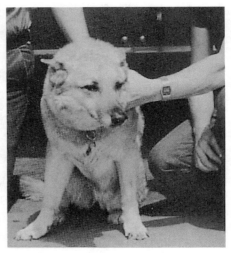

Babe of Engine 101 poses for a yearbook photo (1988).

As they made their approach on Babe, a Boeing 737 waited patiently as the security officers tried to coax the pooch into the car. Eventually, Babe made her way to the car, and the Chicago Police immediately identified the dog as Engine 101's. The police drove the exhausted dog back to the firehouse where she collapsed as soon as she hit Chicago Fire Department cement. For all of the following Fourth of Julys, firefighters gave her tranquilizers during the fireworks displays.

Engine 47

Engine 47, 432 E. Marquette Ave., was home to several mascots that served the city for long stretches of time. *Otis*'s first day on the job occurred on a balmy spring afternoon in 1992 when the crew retrieved him from the scene of a fire. The dog, also known as *Odie*, was tied to the garage of a house that had just burned to the ground. When the firefighters noticed no one had come back to claim him, they all felt sorry for the pooch and voted to take him to the firehouse.

Otis adapted well and became known as a homebody, so the firefighters were surprised to find him missing one day. The police located him wandering the streets and promptly brought him back to Engine 47's quarters. Someone had placed the number "45" on the side of Otis' body. The house later learned that it was Engine 63 who had pulled the stunt, not Engine 45, which made sense because Engine 63 and Engine 47 had a longstanding history of playing pranks on each other.

OTIS RETIRED FROM the department on July 14, 2001, and Engine 47's transition firedog was *Tinkerbell*, a mutt

named after the endearing character in *Peter Pan*. She initially lived at the Engine 47's previous house at 1024 E. 73rd St. for ten years before moving to today's firehouse on Marquette Road. She was the only firedog in Chicago to have a *Sports Illustrated* subscription—the address label had her name on it. Tinkerbell liked to hang out and rest under the wheel wells of

Otis of Engine 47.

the engine. She always knew to get out of the way when the alarm sounded, but several puppies lost their lives trying to imitate her. She died a year after arriving in the new house in 1975 and was buried at 67th and Burnham. An extra headstone was acquired from a local craftsman and the house wrote her name on the headstone with black magic marker. *Stanley* took over and lasted until the early 1980s, eventually weighing over 60 pounds, a lot for a dog who only stood two inches off the ground.

Engine 60

Although many dogs in Chicago firehouses have had the name *Smokey*, each brought their own distinct flavor to the house. The current Smokey at Engine 60, 1150 E. 55th St., is anything but common. She is not only an amazing watchdog but gave birth to one of the largest litters in firedog history.

Brought to the house as a puppy in 1990, Smokey is a 12-year-old, purebred firedog. From the moment she first stepped into the house, she was the center of attention of all the local male dogs. She often spent the afternoon with her suitors, in her pursuit of the right mate. Because she was such a looker, a massive Doberman Pinscher once placed his front paws on the door, looking for Smokey. Not wanting to tussle with the gnarly beast, the men let him sit there for about an hour until boredom overcame him. No doubt he would have recited poetry if given the chance.

For several weeks, the Doberman followed Smokey around. But she was uninterested, and he finally stopped hounding her. After finding the right partner, Smokey became pregnant before her first birthday. That autumn, Smokey began giving birth at 6:30 in the morning and didn't stop until 11:00 that night. One firefighter acted as the midwife, while the rest of the crew slapped each other on the back like proud fathers waiting outside the delivery room in a hospital. After the litter of 12 was born, however, Smokey was spayed.

Smokey has a very specific appetite. If she doesn't like the food for the day, she usually buries it in the backyard. It is customary for the crew to give her a bone from a roast as a treat. When she's done with it, Smokey promptly takes it to the backyard and buries it, which is no problem in the summer, because the crew can easily retrieve it. However, in the winter, she doesn't get too far beneath the frozen earth. Every spring, when the warm weather melts away the snow, the house, as one firefighter reported, looks like a "doggie graveyard with bones sticking half-in and half-out of the ground." For the record, Smokey never buries corned beef on buttered rye bread, a meal she can consume in nothing flat.

Smokey prefers the front lawn of the house to any other spot. She immerses herself in firehouse life—shopping with the cook, playing ball with the kids, and loving every minute of it. One firefighter tried to take Smokey up to his lake house in Michigan, but the homesick dog cried most of the weekend. The firefighter cut the weekend short, and Smokey was delighted to be home again.

SMOKEY HAD A good teacher in her predecessor *Brown Dog*. The two were an inseparable pair. Brown Dog led the way with Smokey trailing, as the duo went for their daily walk to the park. He taught her how to ride the rig and bark at passing pedestrians when the engine was backing in. Brown Dog gladly put up with Smokey's puppy antics like nibbling at his ears and constant poking. He taught her the ways of firehouse life, and it was with great pride that the house adopted Smokey as the firehouse dog when Brown

Smokey protects the rig no matter what.

Dog passed away.

Brown Dog was a beloved member of the crew. The crew once used him to institute an unforgettable prank. The first shift cooked a ham and ate it for dinner. They gave the bone to Brown Dog, who relished his succulent treat, playing with it all day. That evening, the cook prepared a vegetable broth for the second shift. He included the bone for . . . taste. When the second shift arrived in the morning, they were surprised but grateful that the generous cook had prepared their lunch. All the firefighters complimented on the broth's excellent flavor, and Brown Dog once again received the same bone as a treat for his undying service.

Brown Dog rode the rig, falling off regularly because he rode on the very back part

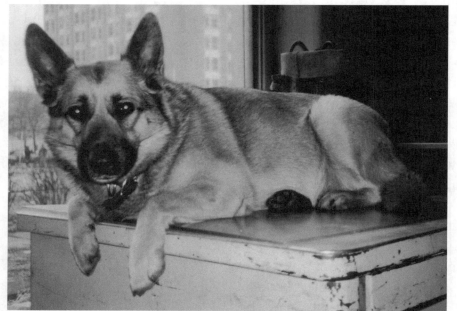

Brown Dog lounging on Engine 60's desk (1993).

of the engine. He also climbed ladders and accompanied men into burning buildings. Legend has it that Brown Dog saved several lives, and although no one knows for sure, the firefighters at Engine 60 have no doubt that he did. The mutt also cruised the neighborhood for several days at a time. He died in 1990, and a firefighter placed a cement plaque into the bricks of the house reading: *A Good Friend—Brown Dog—1976–1990*. A drawing of the dog was placed in the

cement and the memorial stands where the firefighters can see it everyday as a reminder of their faithful sidekick.

Engine 63

Not only did it house one of the oldest-known Chicago firedogs since the blaze of 1871, Engine 63 has had canine crews unique unto themselves. Currently holding court at 1405 E. 62nd Pl. is *Butch II*. The colossal German Shepherd maintains the traditional role of watchdog, and it's a job he does with impeccable force, speed, and accuracy. This area is one of the city's roughest, but under the watchful eye of Butch II, the firefighters sleep a little easier.

Butch II was donated to the house in 1993 and his reputation has not come easy. He's the sheriff of this tough and unforgiving neighborhood. In addition to human intruders, gangs of stray dogs threaten the area. At one time, five vagrant mutts were looking to establish turf near the house, and Butch II wouldn't allow it. A showdown of O.K.-Corral proportions ensued. After the dust settled, Butch II had killed one of the dogs and mauled the remaining four. Butch II also knows the exact property lines of the house, and if an unfamiliar visitor comes too close to the apron, he'll jump right in their face and won't stop until they have retreated.

Everyday after school, he goes out to the fenced-in yard and barks at the passing kids. Butch II could easily go outside the fence and directly confront them, but it's his way of letting them know who is boss of the block. Because of the nine-year-old dog's presence, the firefighters are able to carry out their job with more security and peace of mind. But don't be fooled by his ferocious protectiveness, for he is also magnanimous in his guard dog duties.

Butch II also likes the garbage truck, sprinting towards it as it approaches each week. It's about the only time that he'll cross the firehouse borders and venture into the street. When Butch II catches up to the slow-moving truck, he tries to bite the tires, but they are entirely too large for him to damage. Not so with the chief's car—he's caused at least one flat during his reign.

He has been run over three times, which was miraculously low considering the volume of his chases. The garbage truck ran over his leg, and the crew took him to the vet where he had emergency surgery. Butch II needed five pins to repair the break, and during the recovery, three people were needed to change the bandage twice a week. The firehouse spent over $1,000 on vet bills in order to bring him back to health.

THOUGH NOT IN lineage, Butch II was the progeny of *Butch I*. They were similar in breed, size, and temperament, although the elder Butch was a tad feistier. Butch I lived during the 1970s and was known to stand his ground regardless of circumstance. For instance, when a tiny dog

foolishly tried to attack him, the affair ended with the German Shepherd picking her up in his mouth and shaking her like a rag doll. Five firefighters had to pull Butch off the dog that luckily scampered away uninjured.

If the engine was on a run, Butch was on high alert. Two police officers came by to visit the house, and as they stepped into the station, the cops noticed the engine was gone. Before they could turn to leave, Butch barreled through the kitchen door, pinning the officers against a wall. An hour and a half later, when the engine returned, the two men were still against the wall, soaked in sweat and service pistols drawn.

Butch's services were not always so counterproductive. A burglar had cased the house for several days, tracking the engine's speed in returning, watching the different

Butch II of Engine 63.

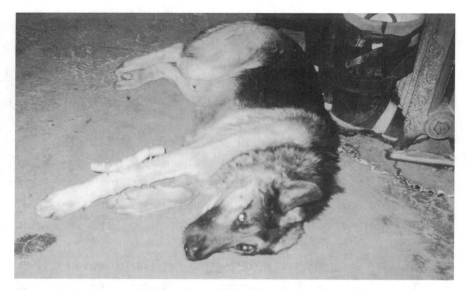

Even with a cast on his leg, Butch II still remained a loyal companion to the crew of Engine 63 (1990).

shifts, and looking in the window for loot. Apparently the guy never saw Butch, for when he finally made the move to rob the house, the dog met him in the house's recreation room. The firemen shortly returned to find Butch barking at the phone booth where the criminal was holed up. Unfortunately, Butch's style proved too hazardous in the long run, and he was put to sleep shortly after he bit a visitor.

ASIDE FROM THE two Butches, a host of other characters inhabited the Hyde Park house. *Susie II* was donated to the house during the 1990s. She frequently jumped out of the firehouse windows for her daily patrols. While the firefighters were eating dinner one evening, they heard a clamorous thud upstairs and ascended to the bunkroom to find that Susie had tried to jump out the window. The only prob-

lem was that the window was closed. Susie wasn't seriously hurt, but she remained dazed for several hours after the mishap. The firefighters couldn't help but chuckle at the thought of Susie running headlong into a closed window.

IN THE 1980S, *Justice* was known for his taste in cigarettes. He would carefully extinguish cigarette butts with his paws and then eat them like little doggy treats. He was eventually stolen from the house.

DURING THE 1960S, the first *Susie* called Engine 63 home. She was deathly afraid of fireworks and hid beneath the engine whenever they went off. On the Fourth of July, Susie couldn't be found. She was easily entertained, however, chasing the beam of a flashlight for hours at a stretch. Susie was the last dog to serve on Maryland Avenue before christening the current house in 1969.

Susie of Engine 63 awaiting her crew (1960).

IN THE 1950S, *Schnapps*, a Collie that was a dead-ringer for *Lassie*, lived at the house when it was located at 6330 S. Maryland Ave., a few blocks from its present location. He was known for two things: eating and riding to fires. Though he didn't mind riding the rig, the plush comfort of the division marshal's car was always the preferred way to go. Bruno reported that the "siren and Schnapps' barking may not sound like much from the back of a big engine, but it's a nerve-shattering experience in an automobile." His beautiful coat and easygoing manner earned him a spot in the finals during the *Chicago American* fire mascot competition.

Engine 64

Engine 64's house moved to its present location at 7659 S. Pulaski Rd. in 1936. That same year, the *Chicago Tribune* provided one of the oldest written accounts of a firedog when they covered *Bum*, "a firemen's dog with a chewed-off ear. A drowsy, frowzy canine with everything in him, from Boston Bull Blood to Collie, Bum has made his home for three years with the boys at Company 64, 6240 S. Laflin St., and hasn't missed a fire."

A firefighter trained Bum to understand the codes that cracked through the joker box. Before electronic devices made firefighting more efficient, the crew had to listen for the ticks that were constantly humming throughout the station. Bum's spot was right beneath the machine. He snoozed, ate, and carried out his day within a few feet of it. He was so adept at discerning the signals that the two interdepartment telephone lines could ring and he could still hear the telegraph line. When he heard the appropriate ticks signaling Engine 64, Bum bolted upright, barked loudly, and made his way aboard the fire wagon. Bum made a few friends in the neighborhood, and if he was playing with them while the engine was rolling out, Bum sprinted toward it and jumped aboard.

Engine 80

Despite being located within the city limits, Engine 80 at 12701 S. Doty Ave. is surrounded by wilderness. With coyotes, possum, raccoons, rabbits, cats, and even wild dogs roaming the nearby woods, the area is more like something from Jack London's *Call of the Wild* than Nelson Algren's *Neon Wilderness*. From this isolated location, Engine 80 acts as a quasi-adoption agency for dogs. The house is a revolving door for unwanted canines, and if some mutt isn't strolling into the quarters, one is being dropped off at the firehouse door. Most of the dogs that have lived at Engine 80 share the common experience of spending only a short time there. A halfway house of sorts, it's up to the crew to care for each dog and keep it out of harm's way until someone adopts it or a firefighter takes it home.

Max was a rather large German Shepherd that found his way to Engine 80 after following the rig for nearly a mile. Seeing that the dog was malnourished, the crew immediately took him in. He was the house garbage disposal, eating everything from rats to the carcass of a turkey—bones and all. Max wanted to sow his wild oats, though; once he found out about girls, he never returned. After Max came *Big Boy*, another German Shepherd who died during the early 1980s of natural causes.

FOLLOWING BIG BOY was *Queenie*, a yellow Lab known

Queenie poses for the yearbook (1988).

for her fierce temperament as a guard dog, but an otherwise quiet demeanor. If not in uniform, a visitor was live bait. One afternoon a firefighter's friend dropped by the house for a quick visit, but the rig was on a run and the station was empty. The only sign of life was a growling Queenie. Finding himself face-to-face with possible bodily harm, the guy ran for his life, finding refuge . . . on top of the refrigerator. The engine returned a half-hour later, and this gentleman was still on top of the fridge. Seeing the friend's position, the crew let him sit for a couple more minutes while he screamed for them to call off Queenie. He was the only one not laughing when he finally got down. Queenie died several years later from natural causes.

QUEENIE'S SUCCESSOR WAS *Blackie*, a purebred mutt that resided at Engine 80 during the 1990s. They nicknamed him Seven because underneath his belly, in white, was a perfectly formed number 7. Blackie loved to chase balls and would do so for the entire day until he either dropped from exhaustion or the fireman's arm wore out.

A bit of a bruiser, Blackie once tangled with a wild raccoon. He ultimately won, leaving the creature with even darker circles around his eyes. But like all the dogs at Engine 80, Blackie didn't last too long. When firefighters

Big Boy of Engine 80 (1980).

weren't looking, he was kidnapped from the apron of the house and never seen again.

Engine 100

The name *Brown Dog* has been given to many mutts throughout the Chicago Fire Department, but the Brown Dog at Engine 100, 6843 S. Harper Ave., was so cherished that his remains were placed in the backyard, and a picture of him still rests above the kitchen cabinets. Brown Dog was an effective guard dog, so efficient at his job that he utilized those skills at fire scenes, chasing anyone who came near the rig. He was an equal opportunity protector; even police officers couldn't escape a snarl. Officers drew their weapons on more than one occasion until a firefighter called him off. Brown Dog's strenuous protection, however, led to several arrests including one in which a would-be intruder fled to the roof of a nearby car to escape an attack.

On one afternoon in the early 1990s, Engine 100 flooded when a pipe burst. After the firemen located and fixed the leak, they heard the familiar howl of Brown Dog emanating from the basement. Two crewmembers ventured down the stairs and found the mutt standing in the water. When they picked Brown Dog up, he immediately stopped howling. But when they set him back down, Brown Dog quickly resumed his sorrowful

Brown Dog in front of Engine 100 (1988).

sound. They later determined that a low voltage charge was running through the water causing him enough discomfort to say something about it. Brown Dog was not hurt in the flooding, living for 15 years before dying of natural causes at the firehouse.

BARRON CAME TO the house in 1973. The big mutt was kept on a chain that was equidistant from the front of the house to the back. Whenever Barron sprinted from one end to the other, the men had to lift up their feet or else the chain bruised them. Rookies got the worst of it, and by the end of their probationary period they usually had severely bruised shins. Not loved by all, Barron was shot and killed in 1979 by a local who couldn't stand the dog's barking.

Engine 28

Nestled in a residential South Side neighborhood stands Engine 28, 2534 S. Throop St., home to *Alex*, from 1977 until his heroic death in 1982. The house continues to service the Bridgeport area, but also answers calls to the Englewood housing projects, among the most notorious high-rise projects in the country. The black Schnauzer was simply known as the *Wonderdog*. Petting this hardworking dog resulted in hands covered with soot and grease. His fur was always dirty due to his unwavering commitment to ride the engine and follow the men into fires. Alex even helped the men pull the hoselines off the rig by gripping the nylon in his teeth and dragging it to the street.

Alex seemed to sense when the alarm was about to broadcast, but it was not so much a sixth sense as acute hearing that gave him the head start to the rig. During this era, firehouse alarms were wired to a central command center on the West Side, and an operator announced the call over a loudspeaker located in the house. The firefighters speculated that Alex was able to hear the initial crack of the speakers just before the operator came on the line. As soon as Alex broke for the rig, the firefighters knew they had a call, giving the engine a split-second advantage. When responding to an alarm, the firefighters oftentimes couldn't slide down the pole because Alex was at the bottom frantically barking at the crew to get moving. They usually took the stairs down to the engine but were once again subjected to the rigorous barking of Alex, encouraging the men to move faster.

Alex was only five years old when he died in the line of duty on July 28, 1982. Engine 28 was responding to a call at 858 N. Orleans St. This fire was not in Engine 28's normal area of responsibility, but the fire was so massive that it required the attention of several companies. As usual, Alex joined the men on the run and went with them into the burning building. He became lost in the blaze, succumbing in the end to smoke inhalation. Former mayor Jane Byrne was so moved by the dog's story that she purchased a plaque that still sits in the front entrance of the house. Mounted on a wooden backboard, the brass memorial reads:

Alex's memorial plaque.

In memory of Alex the Wonderdog. Our buddy aged 5 years gave his life bravely in the line of duty on 7–28–82 when answering a still and box 856 at 0315am at 858 North Orleans. He died true blue with the men he knew, the men with the ladder and the hose. Engine Co. 28 Truck 8.

Mayor Byrne offered to get them a new dog, but the firefighters declined. No dog could replace Alex.

TIMES CHANGED AND during the 1990s, Pamela Lesher was a paramedic on Ambulance 19, which made its home at Engine 28's quarters. Lesher came to the house in 1996 and met the only other female, *Pepper*, a seasoned seven-year-old Dalmatian. As is typical with many firedogs, someone who was moving out of the city gave Pepper to the house.

Lesher and Pepper hit it off immediately, and the paramedic fondly recalled that the dog "slept in my bed and would sit and wait where the ambulance was parked when we went out on a run." Not only a friend to all the firefighters stationed at Engine 28, Pepper frequently visited the neighbors' houses where she was lavished with food and affection. Others came by to take a look at her scrapbook and blue ribbons, which she earned as a show dog before signing up with the department.

Pepper of Engine 28 (1993).

Pepper has since retired and now lives with Lesher and her husband, also a firefighter. The 14-year-old star moves a little slower, but as Lesher put it, she "still has that spirit you never lose once you've lived and worked in a firehouse."

CONNECT-THE-DOTS was another dog that lived at Engine 28; he was killed in the line of duty when he ran under the engine as it was departing for a fire. The firefighters were comforted in knowing that the dog died doing what he loved: being a member of the Chicago Fire Department.

Engine 29

When one thinks of the South Side of Chicago, the Bridgeport neighborhood often comes to mind. It is here that Engine 29, 3509 S. Lowe Ave., makes its quarters. Once the home of both Mayor Daleys, the neighborhood is one of the many backbones of Chicago. This is in the vicinity of the infamous, and now long-gone, stockyards that led Carl Sandburg to call Chicago the "hog butcher of the world." Bridgeport is a working-class neighborhood where you don't dare mention the Cubs favorably. Bridgeport residents were the inspiration for the *Saturday Night Live* skit, the "Superfans," in which characters sit around eating Polish sausages and talking about "Da Bears."

Ashes is the 16-year-old Dalmatian originally given to Engine 29 by a friend of a fireman. She currently holds court in her bed next to the phone booth in the kitchen. When she was a bit sprier, she climbed aboard the rigs and rode with the men on top of the hose bed. Ashes was also known for going into the scenes of fires, often leading the way. If she wandered from the scene, the engineer only had to honk the guttural horn, and no matter where she was, Ashes would sprint back to the rig. As she aged, the men made room for her in the front cab. Today, she no longer accompanies the engine, but every time it comes back from a run, she rises to greet the members like a worried mother who stays up late until her children return from a night out.

Engine 29 also services the Robert Taylor Homes. During the mid-1980s, the Robert Taylor complex was the largest housing project in the country, consisting of 28 high-rise buildings, each 16 stories high. Many fires broke out in the densely-populated complex, which at one time housed over 28,000 residents, and Engine 29 often made runs to extinguish formidable blazes. When the men of Engine 29 went to the Robert Taylor Homes, their only protection was Ashes. She would guard the rig with a fierce sense of loyalty, snarling every time a non-uniformed person came close to the rig. She always kept the men as safe as she could, even in the grimmest of circumstances, willing to sacrifice her life for the lives of the firefighters.

Ashes was also a neighborhood favorite. She roamed the quiet residential streets, making the rounds to many of the houses. Eleanor Daley, the wife of Mayor Richard J.

Ashes in front of Comiskey Park.

Daley, was a fond friend of the dog. People lined up to watch Ashes engage in her favorite pastime: trying to "eat" the water from a flowing hydrant as it sprayed into the street.

With the hydrant pumping at full blast, she liked to jump in front and chow down on the jet stream. The neighborhood kids always asked about Ashes, not really interested in finding out how the firefighters were doing, even if they had just returned from a five-alarm blaze. Ashes frequently rode along with the police officers from the neighboring station in their cruisers, but her true calling was at the firehouse.

Ashes gained quite a bit of notoriety when she was pictured in Firehouse Magazine. When she was later profiled in a children's book about a day in the life of a firedog, she spent a full day at the house being pampered and admired by a professional photographer. She was, after all,

Ashes catches the high-pressure water from a fire hydrant (1995).

a celebrity and had to be treated as such.

Ashes spent many days at Comiskey Park, now U.S. Cellular Field, home of the Chicago White Sox. As a way of saying thanks, the Sox organization often brought the firemen onto the field during the pre-game ceremonies and Ashes always accompanied them. She was available following the national anthem to greet the kids and enjoy a hot dog or two. She loved going to the games, but like most dogs, couldn't stand the fireworks that erupt each time a Sox player hits a homerun. During one game she managed to break free of her leash and started running down the left field line. A firefighter had to chase her down with the help of an Andy Frain usher. When they finally caught her, they were on the stadium's Jumbotron screen and television broadcast. The cameras caught Ashes's rear end in the firefighter's face as he raced back to the stands. The commissioner was so amused that he called the house the next day to extend his personal congratulations.

Today, Ashes takes medicine for her arthritis but still accompanies one of the firefighters to Michigan when he has a day off. The black dots on her fur have faded, but serve as a testament to her 16 years of service. No matter where she goes, however, her true home is still at Engine 29, and as one firefighter said, "There isn't one of us that doesn't love her."

Engine 34

Before moving to its current location at 4034 W. 47th St., Engine 34 and Squad 2 were located at 114 N. Aberdeen St. on Chicago's West Side. The former company was a bastion of firehouse dogs, beginning with *Albert* in the late

1940s. The mutt was brought in by a Skid-Row dweller, and Albert promptly took to life at the house. Although he once fell off the rig, Albert was undeterred in performing his duties.

Albert and the crew of Engine 34 (1954).

Like so many other firehouse dogs, he was tragically killed in the line of duty by a speeding car.

The local papers covered Albert's story, resulting in dozens of offers from citizens to replace the pooch. Rather than write or phone, many actually brought dogs to the house, hoping they might receive the honor of being the house's new firedog. Attempting to heal the loss of their beloved Albert, the crew accepted six dogs and conducted "auditions" to find an adequate replacement.

DOTTIE, YET ONE more contestant donated to the house by a police officer, brought the grand total of qualifiers to seven. The firemen couldn't decide which dog to employ, but the strongwilled, pedigreed Dalmatian Dottie decided for them. The alarm sounded, and six dogs frantically scattered throughout the house. Amidst the canine chaos, Dottie quickly leaped onto the engine, finding an inconspicuous spot in the rear of the rig. The captain reported in the *Chicago American* that "[s]he just seemed to know there was a place for her on the back of the squad wagon. She's been riding there ever since."

Upon returning to the house, the crew gave the remaining six dogs to adoptive families, and Dottie began her formal training at the firehouse. When the bell rang, Dottie learned to be first aboard. When the men were sleeping and the alarm sounded, Dottie awoke the guys with a booming series of barks. Hal Bruno reported that she was most happy performing her tricks, "such as ringing the Waker bell with her paw, flipping dog candy from her nose and catching it in her mouth, retrieving sticks, and carefully stomping out discarded cigarettes without burning her foot."

Before the electronic alarms were installed, the firemen used a "joker" to respond to a call. The joker spat out a series of numbers, and the crew knew to respond to a fire based on the sounds spouted from the intricate system. Engine 34's number was three–four, and after three clicks of the joker, Dottie was off and running to the rig. One firefighter remarked that she could count better than some of the other members in the house.

While serving at the firehouse, Dottie had a litter of puppies. The crew kept one, marking the first in a series of parent–child city servants at the house. *Toughie* and his mother worked well together, and in a short time, Toughie was putting out cigarettes with his paw and riding the rig to fires. The pair became famous when they appeared on *Curley Bradley's Animal Care Time* television show with a pair of turtles. The reptile curator of the Brookfield Zoo demonstrated the contrast between the slow-moving turtles and the swift firehouse dogs.

THE COMPANY ALSO housed the golden Labradors *Bozo* and *Bozo, Jr.* Like Dottie with Toughie, Bozo instructed Bozo Junior on the ways of life in a Chicago firehouse. The crew saw numerous dogs go through the station door, most of them mutts with no distinguishable breed. But, as one firefighter stated of all the dogs, "We consider them thoroughbreds."

The house at 114 N. Aberdeen St. was eventually abandoned and the company moved to the South Side at 4034 W. 47th St. Although the crew has not recently adopted any dogs, they did make room for *Jane* in the 1990s. Jane was a white goose known for her fierce loyalty and ardent service. She didn't last too long, however, and one of the firemen took her home after the house realized geese were tough to toilet train.

Engine 39

Chicago Sun-Times reporter Mark Brown described Engine 39 as "a little one truck firehouse that time forgot." Indeed, the house is surrounded by residential structures and sits tucked away from the intersection of Ashland Avenue and 33rd Place. Across the street is a playground where local families go with their children during the summers. Because of its proximity to the station, the small park provides the ideal place for many of the residents to become acquainted with the firefighters, and a casual and friendly relationship has developed over the years. Several dogs inhabited the station over a span of 50 years, and their presence has always added to the neighborhood's congenial feeling.

The setting at 1618 W. 33rd Pl. has not changed much over the last few decades, but the serene atmosphere was briefly riddled with controversy by the exodus of *Slate*, Engine 39's firehouse dog. Mark Brown wrote of Slate's banishment on September 7, 2000, and the framed article sits in Engine 39's kitchen—a gentle reminder of more innocent times.

Slate was also known as *Rigsby* or *Blackie* depending on the shift. The fun-loving black Labrador with a bit of Rottweiler was the mascot of Engine 39 for a number of years. Unlike some of his firedog peers, Slate did not do anything heroic during his tenure. He didn't ride the rig, and he certainly didn't go into fires. Slate was deathly afraid of water and as Brown wrote, "preferred to wait patiently at the firehouse for the crew to return." Slate tried to protect the house with ferocious barking when the crew was away on a call, but according to Brown, he did not "possess the character traits required of most real firehouse dogs, which is to say that he wasn't mean and vicious." Though he looked tough, he never barked at other dogs or the unfamiliar citizens who frequently dropped by the house. In short, Slate was a sweet pet who enjoyed a dog's life in a Chicago firehouse.

Sparky looks at his oil painting —he was the official symbol for fire protection (1958).

Slate quickly developed a well-settled routine of eating and sleeping in between the alarms that shrieked throughout the station. The dog's forte was with the neighborhood children who, according to Brown, "regularly dropped by to play with Slate . . . or he crossed the street to visit them in the local play lot—which may be where the trouble started." An overworried mother put the screws on Slate by filing an official complaint with the city. Concerned about the safety of her children while Slate was at the playground, the woman obtained an order from Engine 39's department supervisor that Slate be chained and muzzled at all times. The firemen couldn't fathom enforcing that kind of treatment, but they nonetheless tried.

Ironically, Slate's imprisonment was practically his downfall. The firefighters reluctantly put the dog on a long chain, fastened to the fence in the backyard. Slate became entangled in the mass, and the chain wound up around his neck, choking him. The cook noticed Slate in the backyard, unmoving, nearly lifeless. He rushed out, began CPR, and successfully revived Slate. The firefighters decided that the leash was, after all, not a good idea.

According to Brown's piece, a neighbor insisted that "[h]e's pretty much a neighborhood dog . . . I've never heard of him biting, scratching or even barking at any of the kids. He's not a vicious dog, or I wouldn't have him around my kids." The neighbor ended the dispute by buying Slate for a dollar. While the neighbor's gesture allowed him to have a "different" owner and address, Slate couldn't deny his firedog blood. Slate's new owner assured the department supervisor that he would distance him from the firehouse, though he frequently forgot to lock the gate to the fence where Slate resided. Naturally, Slate wandered back over to the firehouse to be reunited with his crew.

This routine persisted for a couple of weeks without incident, but the arrangement couldn't last forever. The cranky mother no doubt placed a call to the department upon seeing a free Slate strolling around the house and continually spending time at the playground. To make matters worse, a surprise visit by the supervisor found Slate lingering in the backyard of the station, eagerly awaiting lunch. The irate chief immediately pounded on the "owner's"

door, commanding him to leash Slate. If he didn't comply, he would personally escort Slate to the pound.

The neighbor's daughter had recently viewed a PBS special on what happens to naughty pooches who go to the pound. If not adopted, they are sent to the execution chamber. The neighbor's rage sparked him to speak with the *Sun-Times* reporter, and Brown's stinging article quickly followed. Not wanting to see the loyal Slate killed, the neighbor gave Slate to one of the firefighters who took him home. The local residents still allow their dogs to roam free around the playground, but something is amiss. To this day, Slate has never returned, and we are left wondering why bad things happen to good dogs.

ENGINE 39 WASN'T always home to controversy. Aside from having a massive Saint Bernard during the early 1980s, the station was home to several dogs during the 1950s. *Duke*, a massive Dalmatian, often rode the rig with the men. Not every call was a fire; once the men were dispatched to clean an acid spill after a semitruck collided with a car on Archer and Western Avenues. Duke normally wandered at the scene of an incident, and that day was no exception. However, Duke seared the bottom of his paws when he stepped into the highly corrosive acid. The firemen rushed Duke to the animal hospital. The veterinarian believed his injuries were fatal and urged the men to put the dog to sleep. The beleaguered crew refused and spent the next two weeks bathing Duke's wounded feet every hour on the hour. Because of the men's will and vigilance, Duke healed completely. But after the incident, he left the firefighting to his crew, staying on the engine whenever the men answered a call.

Sparky succeeded Duke as the house's mascot in 1958. Another Dalmatian, he was an avid protector of the rig. Sparky became the official symbol of fire protection and poster dog for the 1959 department calendar. An artist was commissioned to paint an oil portrait of the dog for the fire safety campaign. From all accounts, Sparky approved of the portrait and accepted responsibility of his new collateral job.

Engine 41

Chicago holds the honor of maintaining the world's largest municipal harbor system, with over 60 miles of riverfront winding through the city and over 20 miles of Lake Michigan shoreline circumscribing Chicago's eastern boundary. There has always been a need for the Chicago Fire Department to maintain a strong presence on Lake Michigan and the Chicago River. Despite attempts to develop seafaring qualities, no dog has ever been bred to withstand the challenges of a maritime environment because the constant and unpredictable motions of any marine platform incapacitate most dogs. Even the U.S. Coast Guard prohibits the retention of dogs aboard vessels for extended periods, despite their unparalleled ability to detect drugs and explosive substances. It takes a special kind of puppy to be a true "seadog," and only two Chicago firedogs have ever served on the water.

During the 1950s, Hal Bruno reported on *Skippy*, who served on the now-retired *Fred A. Busse* fireboat, a vessel docked at the harbor just north of the Throop Street Bridge. While the other firedogs preferred the terra firma of the firehouse, Skippy chose a different route—one that would

take him all over the city via the Chicago River and Lake Michigan. The fireboat only got underway for special fires, drills, or assisting the Coast Guard in search and rescue cases, so Skippy had more free time than most firedogs. If the work was completed for the day, Skippy walked over to the battalion headquarters a few blocks from the waterfront at 918 W. 19th St. and spent his time making rounds with

Skippy of Engine 41 (1955).

the battalion chiefs to the various firehouses in the district. Also serving the water community was a pooch from Engine 58. In the 1910s, the dog supported the fire hose wagon at the 95th Street Bridge. In their book, *History of Chicago Fire Houses of the 19th Century*, Ken Little and John McNallis explained, Engine 58's "crew operated this two horse wagon which consisted of a large hose reel mounted inside a plain wagon. The reel carried 3-1/2-inch hose and the hose wagon would lead it out from the fireboat to the fire, supplying water for hand lines or a street pipe . . ." When the dog was not helping firefighters pull the boat off the wagon, he was rumored to enjoy spear fishing (using his mouth) for fresh fish.

Engine 50

Engine 50 at 5000 S. Union Ave. was home to many dogs, including a very rare breed never seen before in a Chicago firehouse. In the 1960s, the firemen were coming home from a call and they saw what appeared to be a very small dog on a leash held by a young man. The firefighter offered to give the young man $20 for the animal, but the owner immediately asked for $35. The firefighter agreed and executed the transaction, expecting to get reimbursed by the guys at the house. When they returned, he collected $2 from everyone, but a relief Lieutenant named Billy refused to pay because he wasn't a full-time member of Engine 50. When they offered to name the new addition after him, the LT was persuaded. So they called him *Billy*—or *Billy Goat* to be more specific. Any relationship to Chicago's famous Billy Goat Tavern was a complete coincidence.

Billy Goat once occupied the confines of Engine 50 (1963).

The firefighters called the front office and asked if there was a problem keeping a goat, and they received specific instructions not to let him bother the neighbors. So the baby Billy goat lived at Engine 50 for over six months. They nourished him with goat feed that the firefighters purchased during their vacations to Wisconsin. The neighborhood kids nicknamed him *Devil Dog* because of his large horns, and the firefighters permitted ramming sessions with the couch cushions. Billy didn't ride on the rig like other firedogs, but he did do other services regular dogs couldn't perform. Billy mowed the house's lawn, cutting the small patch of grass next to the house. He also ate the ticker tape from the joker. Billy eventually outgrew the house and was donated to a children's farm off Chicago's Southwest Highway.

JIGGS WAS AN enormous Bulldog who stood post in the 1970s. He was usually tied up to the stand holding the old "Running Cards"—the cards showing a planned response with specific equipment to a particular area—and the chain had just enough range to take him to the door. One night, two kids came into the house looking for trouble. The kids took one look at the dog and sprinted out of the house. Jiggs was irritated at being awakened and bolted for the kids, taking the Running Cards with him. It was quite a scene to see these cards bouncing down Union Street. Jiggs was only able to go a couple of blocks before he ran out of gas. While the kids were never caught, they never saw the inside of Engine 50 again. The firefighters had to fall behind and retrieve all the cards.

THE YEAR 1980 saw the advent of *Dynamite Lascivious Luster*. The Pit Bull was also known as *Lewd & Lascivious* or simply *Lewd*, and dog-loving *Tribune* columnist Anne Keegan quoted the captain of Engine 50 as saying "he had the ugliest face of any dog on Earth. The face was mean and ugly. And he barked a lot. But I never saw him hurt anyone. I don't think he would." His big teeth and swaggering gait masked his good nature, making him a shrewd protector of the South Side firehouse.

However, the neighborhood was formidable, and on two separate occasions, even the mighty Lewd couldn't defend himself. The first occurred when the men were on a run, and a local resident lured Lewd into his car. The firemen returned, and after a few minutes noticed their dog was missing. They spent the next hour casing the neighborhood, questioning neighbors, and following leads. The firemen finally discovered who took the dog. Numerous witnesses had seen a guy coax Lewd into a car, and from their description, the firemen knew the perpetrator. The thief had a reputation for "hounding" the firemen, and a few members of the crew ventured off to find him. They knocked on his apartment door, and when the door opened Lewd quickly ran toward the waiting firemen. The police were right behind them, leaving the thief to rue the day he messed with Lewd.

Unfortunately, Lewd was stolen again a month later. Knowing the dog's reputation for protection, burglars took the dog in advance to ensure that they had an easy score the next time the rig departed for action. The thieves stole $1,000 in cash from the firefighter's lockers, a $400 color television, and $270 in firehouse funds, as well as the captain's typewriter, clock radio, and small television. They tried to get into the soda machine but gave up, leaving a crowbar in the change slot. The perpetrators left their fingerprints at the scene and were eventually caught. Most of the house's property was returned, but best of all, their prize possession, Lewd, made it safely home.

FOLLOWING LEWD WAS a Beagle named *Denny*. In the 1990s, *Big Ed* followed Denny. Known for his watchdogging, the brown mutt suffered terrible hip and shoulder problems. The vet quoted corrective surgery at about $1,500, without a guarantee of recovery, and the men decided life would be better for Big Ed if he were on the other side. One of the paramedics took him to the vet in the ambulance, and Big Ed was laid to rest a short time later.

SINBAD WAS KNOWN for his evil streak, and the crew nicknamed him *Devil Dog* because he would actually try to stop the guys from leaving the house on the rig. If one of the crew were watching television and the alarm sounded, the dog began to growl, leaving the fireman trapped. The remedy was to have one firefighter distract Sinbad while another pulled the dog away so the stranded member could make the rig.

CURRENTLY, *JOYCE* RESIDES at Engine 50. Named after the current commissioner, the part Rottweiler, part Doberman is just a puppy. He came from a litter spawned by a former firedog—a perfect formula for the making of a thoroughbred firehouse dog. Joyce entered the house on the heels of *Lester*, a Collie hit by a car on May 31, 2001.

Named after the current commissioner, Joyce is a loyal member of Engine 50.

Sinbad's memorial mural adorns the walls of the firehouse.

Repair Shops

The Chicago Fire Department repair shops at 31st and Sacramento have serviced the department's engines, trucks, and ambulances since 1922. The city recently turned the operation over to contractors. In the 1940s, *Nellie* made her home there for over ten years. Puppies from her 14 litters (over 100 puppies) were given to various firehouses throughout the city. Nellie was ten years old when she gave birth one last time to a single pup. The maintenance workers kept Nellie's last child and named him *Butch*. He was schooled by mom and went on to replace her in the early 1950s.

Engine 54

Engine 54, 7101 S. Parnell Ave., has been home to several dogs throughout the years. Because of the often dangerous surroundings, the house employed mean dogs to guard the quarters. In the mid-1970s, a Doberman Pinscher of the junkyard variety was known for his rigorous security procedures. If anyone tried to enter the house in civilian clothes, *Duke* refused entry by either chasing them out of the house or stopping them at the door with loud, ferocious barks. *Larry*, a German Shepherd, had similar traits and worked during the mid-1980s and throughout the 1990s. However, he crossed the line one too many times with his aggressive behavior and had to be put to sleep.

Finally, Engine 54 employed the help of a strapping Saint Bernard during the 1980s. One summer afternoon, the dog was stolen from the house. Several hours later a local resident entered the quarters and claimed to know the captor's hideout but would only tell for a price of $50. The firefighters refused to pay the ransom and told the guy to keep the dog, knowing that the cost of maintaining the gigantic Saint Bernard would bring him back within a few days. Sure enough, three days later, the crew found the dog outside the firehouse door, with a note attached to his collar reading: *You can feed him.*

Lester's headstone.

Hook and Ladder 33

The 1952 presidential election was one of only two times between 1932 and 1968 that the Republican Party won a spot in the White House. That November, former General Dwight D. Eisenhower walloped Adlai Stevenson in a landslide victory. The GOP's success was supported by *Cactus*, a Beagle stationed at Hook and Ladder 33, then located at 4459 S. Marshfield Ave.

While going for a walk with his owner during a crisp

October evening, Cactus came upon a member of the Illinois Labor Youth League illegally stuffing pamphlets into the neighborhood mailboxes. The literature denounced Ike's Far Eastern foreign policy, and Cactus apparently took offense. Although the South Side of Chicago is known for its democratic machine politics where you "vote early and vote often," the conservative Cactus attacked the man, and the firefighter tried to pull him away. Knowing he was in trouble, the teen took off running. On Election Day, the local voting booths were held at Hook and Ladder 33's house. The firefighters stood a careful watch, hoping that the young man would not tempt fate again. Fortunately for him, he was wise enough to abstain from voting that year.

Cactus arrived as a stray puppy, in poor health and on the brink of death. If it were not for the care and attention Cactus received from the men, he would have surely died. After several months of gaining strength, Cactus made a habit of riding to fires in Truck 33's cab. Cactus made all the calls, even when playing with neighborhood children. If he heard the siren, he immediately stopped and raced to get on the truck before it was out of reach. In his free time, Cactus also chased rats in the neighboring stockyards, later attempting to hone those skills on young hippies.

Air and Sea Rescue

The Chicago Fire Department's former Air and Sea squads operated from the heights of Chicago skyscrapers to the cold waters of Lake Michigan. The units usually worked in tandem, spotting victims in the lake from a helicopter overhead and then alerting a surface vessel of their locations. The helicopter was stationed at Meigs Field, and the speedboat was moored at the yacht harbor in Jackson Park.

Star and *Beau* assisted the aircrews in the 1980s, occasionally even saving several of their canine brethren by spotting them from the sky. Indifferent dog owners sometime threw their unwanted pets into the Chicago River where the walls were too high for dogs to climb out. The Air and Sea Rescue crews saved numerous such victims before they became hypothermic and drowned.

Star of the Air and Sea Rescue Squad (1988).

LADY SERVED ON the department's jet boat that made frequent rescues and regular runs for the SCUBA teams. Despite her obvious K9 affiliation as a German Shepherd, she never let a police officer near the boat during the 1970s. But firefighters, even new ones, never had a problem getting aboard. Lady also guarded the quarters and thrived on killing rats in the nearby park. She wasn't present for one rescue when the jet boat came upon a drowning dog that was so exhausted he was at the point of death. As the Afghan went under, a firefighter grabbed him by his coat. The dog was lucky to have had long hair, otherwise the firefighter probably would

Beau of the Air and Sea Rescue Squad (1988).

Lady works and plays with the members of the Air and Sea Rescue Squad (1970).

have lost his grip. The fire-fighter then revived the lifeless pooch by pushing on his chest and clearing the water out of the dog's airway.

Engine 74

Another *Bozo* lived in a Chicago firehouse in the 1950s. This mutt retired after eight years of service at Engine 74's house at 10615 S. Ewing Ave. The old, chubby dog just didn't have the zip needed for the long jump from pavement to the rig's running board. Bozo was able to slim down after spending a week at the pound, but as soon as he returned to the house, his appetite got the best of him. Sometimes firedogs have a tough transition into the civil-ian world, and even though he was forced into early retirement, Bozo caught at least one cab to check out a fire after he was just too big to get on the rig.

Bozo of Engine 74 (1954).

Engine 73

Engine 73, 8630 S. Emerald Ave., was home to *Casey* and *Tonto*, who used some unusual security measures. In the early 1970s, Casey employed the alternative tactic of allowing visitors into the house but never letting them out. Casey used this technique on a robber who shot and killed the dog after Casey refused to let him out. Casey was buried in the back of the house, and another German Shepherd named Tonto picked up where she left off. This

Sarge of Engine 73 (1988).

Shepherd also went to great lengths to keep guests and sometimes even firefighters from leaving. As soon as Tonto saw visitors make a move for the door, he tried to beat them there, growling as if to show his displeasure at their departure. Firefighters frequently had to restrain Tonto so people could leave. *Sarge* replaced Tonto in the late 1980s and despite his law enforcement name, no one could verify exactly what defense strategy he incorporated.

Engine 45

Few other houses in the city can claim that they have buried more dogs than Engine 45 at 4600 S. Cottage Grove Ave. More full-dress funerals have been performed here than any other firehouse in the city. Perhaps the most beloved was *Prairie Dawg*, a German Shepherd that served at the house for six years. The following biography of Prairie ran in the firefighter's Local–2 monthly bulletin, *The Sounder*:

> *Name: Prairie Dawg*
> *Title: Fire Dog*
> *Assignment: Engine 45*
> *Length of Service: 126 years (6 years x's 7 dog years x's 3–24hr shifts with no days off)*

Prairie entered the fire service right after the strike in 1980 and discharged his duties quite admirably since then. Although Prairie Dawg has watched several of his comrades fall in the line of duty (*Sarge*, 1983; *Harold*, 1984; *Rose*, 1985) and been the recipient of numerous Purple Hearts and commendations, he has never let adversity interfere with the performance of his duty. A real dog's dog!

He was found two doors from the house, living on a mattress in an abandoned lot, or prairie as it is often called in Chicago. He absolutely refused to allow anyone within two feet of him; it took a long time before firefighters could approach the dog. But Prairie learned to trust the firehouse and the men who lived there, eventually following his favorite firefighters home after their shift was over. Prairie was known to keep pace with their departing cars, waiting at each light, running for numerous blocks before he was either overcome by exhaustion or outrun.

Prairie was definitely a city dog; his coat always stunk and many of the guys only petted him with gloves because they couldn't wash the smell off their hands. To give him a change of scenery, one of the firefighters took him pheasant hunting in the country. When Prairie arrived, he tip-toed throughout the wooded areas because he had never experienced soil—his whole world had been concrete, asphalt, and broken glass.

Prairie once went missing in action for about a week. The guys speculated that he was struck by a car and would never be seen again. Just as the house was getting ready to abandon hope, they got a run at 43rd Street and Lake Park. They were investigating the scene when Prairie magically materialized from a hidden corner. He ran full speed for the rig when he heard the siren and saw the oscillating lights. They had to hold him down in the cab of the rig because he was so excited to see everybody.

Prairie Dawg was known to get into trouble with the local canine crowd. Usually he won, but even the best of the best lose a few, and Prairie sustained life-threatening injuries after a long scuffle with a rogue dog. Prairie was driven to the University of Illinois School of Veterinarian Medicine, where he was treated to the tune of $1,000. To pay for Prairie's medical bills, the house held a benefit to help defray the costs. The house made T-shirts and raised over $2,000 from the local community. The remaining $1,000 was used for veterinarian follow-ups.

In 1986, Prairie Dawg was injured at the scene of a fire and never made a full recovery. The Local #2 Firefighter's Union

The official logo of Prairie Dawg's fundraiser.

published the following obituary:

> *Local 2 wishes to extend its heartfelt sympathies to the Brothers of Engine #45 on the recent loss of Prairie Dog, who passed away in quarters after a short illness. Prairie Dog responded to a fire where he took a bad beating and three days later passed away. Prairie, like his predecessor, Sarge, were legends both on the fire department as well as with the neighbors along Cottage Grove. Both were Local #2 members. Gone But Not Forgotten. Prairie's life long firefighter friend from Engine 60, Brown Dog, tells about spending many tough winter nights with Prairie, Sarge and himself. Brown says he's joining the rest of all the firehouse mutts, Tinker-Bell, Stanley, Butch, Muggs, Firedog, Dudley, Snoopy, and Rufus at the big apparatus floor in the sky.*

The house loved Prairie so much they wanted to remember him forever, so they looked into getting him stuffed. While they were investigating the option with a taxidermist, one of the firefighters kept the body in an extra freezer he had at home. After they realized it was too expensive, they decided to bury him in the same abandoned lot that he originally called home. They had a funeral service, complete with internment and a full-dress procession to the place of burial. Many local residents attended the service, and firemen placed remembrances on the casket. Following the burial, the neighbors clapped—everyone was deeply moved by the service. A few weeks later, a plaque was also forged into the bricks of the house.

PRAIRIE DAWG'S FOSTER father was *Sarge*, a German Shepherd that came on the scene in 1978. While the details of his life were obscure, his tragic ending was not. Sarge was killed in the line of duty after a United Parcel Service truck ran him over on May 4, 1983. Again, full honors were accorded, and

Sarge of Engine 45 (1983).

Prairie Dawg attended his father's funeral service along with a neighborhood congregation led by the fire chaplain. As usual, the mahogany casket and other arrangements were

At Prairie Dawg's funeral service, his casket was draped with an American flag (1986).

all furnished at the firefighters' expense.

THE HOUSE HAD several other dogs too—*Rose*, named after the captain's wife, in 1985, and *Harold*, the year before. A black Labrador named *Duchess* stayed with one firefighter on every shift in the 1990s. Several mutts served in the 1930s and 1940s, including a dog named *Old Zip*.

Index by Firehouse

♨ Index by Firehouse ♨

The following index includes only the dogs confirmed by the authors to have served in Chicago. Details about the dogs are provided on the page numbers listed, however, not all dogs indexed were featured (n.f.). The time frame refers to the decade in which the firedogs lived, although more specific dates may be provided in the preced-ing pages. Some units/addresses may no longer be in serv-ice. This roster only accounts for a limited percentage of dogs that served in Chicago Fire Department's history. The tomb of the unknown dog in Engine 95's graveyard is just one reminder of the countless undocumented canines that served in the Chicago Fire Department.

Abbreviations:
ASR=Air–Sea Rescue
CFA=Chicago Fire Academy
E=Engine
FS=Flying Squad
HL=Hook and Ladder

IP=Insurance Patrol
P=Patrol
RP=Repair Shops
S=Squad
SS=Snorkel Squad
T=Truck

Co.	Address	Firedog	Timeframe	Pages
E1	220 S. Franklin	Name Unknown	1870s	n.f.
E1	220 S. Franklin	Name Unknown	1870s	n.f.
E1	419 S. Wells	Willie	1970s	92–93
FS1	8701 S. Escanaba	Lady	1950s	n.f.
FS1	8701 S. Escanaba	Dudley	1970s	n.f.
S1	209 N. Dearborn	Lady	1950s	50
S1	209 N. Dearborn	Oz-Dal Lady of Flame	1960s	51
SS1	1044 N. Orleans	Omar	1960s	41–44
SS1	1044 N. Orleans	Zimm	1970s	43–44
SS1	1044 N. Orleans	Fritz	1970s	44–45
IP1	100 S. Desplaines	Chico	1950s	n.f.
IP1	100 S. Desplaines	Brownie	1950s	n.f.
E2	2421 S. Lowe	Dottie	1930s	109
E2	2421 S. Lowe	Bruno	1930s	6, 8, 109
E2	2421 S. Lowe	Name Unknown	1940s	n.f.
E2	2421 S. Lowe	Smokey	1950s	75, 109
E2	2421 S. Lowe	Yick	1950s	108–109
S2	114 N. Aberdeen	Albert	1940s	128–129
S2	114 N. Aberdeen	Dottie	1950s	8, 9,129–130
S2	114 N. Aberdeen	Toughie	1950s	129
S2	114 N. Aberdeen	Bozo, Jr.	1950s	129
S2	114 N. Aberdeen	Bozo	1950s	129
S3	5349 S. Wabash	Name Unknown	1920s	n.f.
S3	5349 S. Wabash	Name Unknown	1940s	n.f.
S3	5349 S. Wabash	Muggs	1950s	112
S3	5349 S. Wabash	Brownie	1960s	n.f.
HL3	158 W. Erie	Nardi	1950s	8, 16, 51–53
E4	548 W. Division	Cleo	1970s	40
E4	548 W. Division	Bear	1980s	39–40
E4	548 W. Division	Eddie	1980s	40
E4	548 W. Division	Tower	1980s	40
E4	1244 N. Halsted	Lucky	1950s	n.f.
S4	1219 W. Gunnison	Mike	1950s	61–62
E5	324 S. Des Plaines	Name Unknown	1910s	n.f.
E5	324 S. Des Plaines	Nellie	1930s	n.f.
E5	324 S. Des Plaines	Tommy	1950s	90–91

Co.	Address	Firedog	Timeframe	Pages	Co.	Address	Firedog	Timeframe	Pages
E57	2412 W. Haddon	Name Unknown	1910s	n.f.	E73	8630 S. Emerald	Sarge	1980s	137, 139
E57	1244 N. Western	Rufus	1970s	15, 93–94	E73	8630 S. Emerald	Tonto	1980s	137
E57	1244 N. Western	Bishop	1980s	n.f.	E74	10615 S. Ewing	Bozo	1950s	137
E58	95th Street Bridge	Name Unknown	1910s	n.f.	E75	6240 S. Peoria	Name Unknown	1920s	n.f.
E59	5714 N. Ridge	Rudy	1980s	62–63	E75	11958 S. State	Rusty	1980s	n.f.
E60	1150 E. 55th	Smokey	1980s	110–111, 118–119	E76	3517 W. Cortland	Smokey	1950s	59
					E76	1747 N. Pulaski	Stormy	1970s	57–58
E60	1150 E. 55th	Brown Dog	1990s	119–120, 139	E76	1747 N. Pulaski	Duke	1970s	59
					E76	1747 N. Pulaski	Stormy II	1980s	58–59
E60	1150 E. 55th	Smokey II	2000s	n.f.	E77	1224 S. Komensky	Name Unknown	1950s	n.f.
E61	5349 S. Wabash	Chance	1920s	112	E77	1224 S. Komensky	Blackie	1960s	75
E61	5349 S. Wabash	Brownie	1960s	111	E77	1224 S. Komensky	Teddy	1970s	n.f.
E61	5349 S. Wabash	Christy	1990s	n.f.	E77	1224 S. Komensky	Duke	1980s	n.f.
E61	5349 S. Wabash	Ashes	2000s	110–111	E78	1052 W. Waveland	Pat	1950s	36
E62	34 E. 114th	Deputy Dog	1980s	112–113	E78	1052 W. Waveland	Spike	1960s	35–36
E62	34 E. 114th	Mutley	1980s	112–113	E78	1052 W. Waveland	Buster	1970s	34, 35
E62	34 E. 114th	Otis	2000s	113–114	E78	1052 W. Waveland	Scotty	1980s	35
E63	6330 S. Maryland	Name Unknown	1890s	n.f.	E78	1052 W. Waveland	Boots	1990s	33–35
E63	6330 S. Maryland	Schnapps	1950s	8, 123	E79	6424 N. Lehigh	Sheeba	1970s	n.f.
E63	6330 S. Maryland	Susie	1960s	122–123	E80	12701 S. Doty	Max	1970s	123
E63	6330 S. Maryland	Susie II	1960s	122	E80	12701 S. Doty	Queenie	1980s	123–124
E63	1405 E. 62nd Place	Butch I	1970s	121–122	E80	12701 S. Doty	Big Boy	1980s	124
E63	1405 E. 62nd Place	Justice	1980s	122	E80	12701 S. Doty	Blackie	1990s	124
E63	1405 E. 62nd Place	Butch II	2000s	120–121	E82	817 E. 91st	Snoopy	1970s	n.f.
E64	6240 S. Laflin	Bum	1930s	123	E83	1200 W. Wilson	Schlitz	1970s	61
E64	7659 S. Pulaski	Name Unknown	1990s	n.f.	E83	1200 W. Wilson	Wino	1980s	9, 28, 59–61
E66	2858 W. Fillmore	Bozo	1950s	75–76	E83	1200 W. Wilson	Wino, Jr.	1990s	61, 62–63
E66	2858 W. Fillmore	Big Red	1960s	76	E84	5721 S. Halsted	Fanny	1920s	115
E67	4666 W. Fulton	Rocky	1970s	68	E84	5721 S. Halsted	Satan	1960s	115–116
E67	4666 W. Fulton	Goofy	1970s	68–69	E84	5721 S. Halsted	King	1970s	116
E68	1642 N. Kostner	Brownie	1950s	94	E84	5721 S. Halsted	Daisy	1970s	116
E68	1642 N. Kostner	Whiskey	1970s	94–95	E84	6204 S. Green	Muggs	1970s	114–115
E70	1545 W. Rosemont	Mickey	1940s	59	E84	6204 S. Green	Sam	1980s	115
E70	1545 W. Rosemont	Beau	1970s	59	E84	6204 S. Green	Rambo	1980s	115
E73	8630 S. Emerald	Casey	1970s	137	E84	6204 S. Green	Jake	1980s	115

Co.	Address	Firedog	Timeframe	Pages	Co.	Address	Firedog	Timeframe	Pages
E84	6204 S. Green	Shep	2000s	115	E101	2240 W. 69th	Babe	1980s	117–118
E84	6204 S. Green	Shredder	2000s	115	E101	2240 W. 69th	Irene/Pepper/Pee-Dog	1990s	116–117
E85	3700 W. Huron	Bambi	1950s	87–88	E103	25 S. Laflin	Bum	1950s	75, 109
E85	3700 W. Huron	Bullets	1960s	88	E103	25 S. Laflin	Matches	1970s	75
E85	3700 W. Huron	Lady	1970s	88	E103	25 S. Laflin	Arson	1980s	70
E85	3700 W. Huron	Seamus	1970s	88	E103	25 S. Laflin	Lady	1990s	69–70
E89	4456 N. Knox	Name Unknown	1930s	n.f.	E103	25 S. Laflin	Bones	1990s	70–71
E89	3945 W. Peterson	Name Unknown	1940s	n.f.	E103	25 S. Laflin	Lugnut	2000s	71–74
E93	330 W. 104th	Sam	1980s	n.f.	E104	1401 S. Michigan	Tim O'Reilly	1950s	103–104
E95	4000 W. Wilcox	Smokey	1950s	79	E106	3401 N. Elston	Cutie	1970s	n.f.
E95	4000 W. Wilcox	Madchen	1970s	79	E107	1101 S. California	Name Unknown	1980s	n.f.
E95	4005 W. West End	Sydney	1980s	79	E107	1101 S. California	Name Unknown	1990s	n.f.
E95	4005 W. West End	Gretta	1980s	80	E107	1101 S. California	Dobby	2000s	n.f.
E95	4005 W. West End	Zulu	1980s	80	E109	2358 S. Whipple	Janie	1970s	n.f.
E95	4005 W. West End	Frankie	1980s	79, 80	E111	1701 N. Washtenaw	Rusty	1950s	n.f.
E95	4005 W. West End	Susie	1980s	80	E111	1701 N. Washtenaw	Name Unknown	1960s	n.f.
E95	4005 W. West End	Pete	1980s	80	E113	5212 W. Harrison	Leroy	1970s	89
E95	4005 W. West End	Blackie	1980s	80	E113	5212 W. Harrison	Name Unknown	1980s	n.f.
E95	4005 W. West End	Shemp	1990s	80	E113	5212 W. Harrison	Lulu	2000s	88–89
E95	4005 W. West End	Lady	1990s	80	E114	3542 W. Fullerton	Tiger	1970s	87
E95	4005 W. West End	Simba	1990s	81	E115	11940 S. Peoria	Kelly	1980s	103
E96	439 N. Waller	Lady	1970s	97–99	E115	11940 S. Peoria	Name Unknown	1990s	n.f.
E96	439 N. Waller	Ernie	1980s	97	E115	11940 S. Peoria	Hobo's Mom	1990s	n.f.
E96	439 N. Waller	Janie	1980s	97	E115	11940 S. Peoria	Hobo	2000s	102–103
E96	439 N. Waller	Max	1990s	n.f.	E115	11940 S. Peoria	Teesha	2000s	102–103
E96	439 N. Waller	Sydney	2000s	96–97	E116	5955 S. Ashland	Diablo	1990s	n.f.
E96	439 N. Waller	Blue	2000s	95–97	E116	5955 S. Ashland	Salty	2000s	104
E97	13359 S. Burley	Wolfie	2000s	n.f.	E117	816 N. Laramie	Penny	1970s	89
E98	202 E. Chicago	Libby Boy	1940s	n.f.	E117	4900 W. Chicago	Brandy	1980s	89–90
E99	3042 S. Kedvale	Bandit	1970s	n.f.	E117	4900 W. Chicago	Petey	1980s	n.f.
E99	3042 S. Kedvale	Peewee	1990s	n.f.	E117	4900 W. Chicago	Ginger	1990s	90
E99	3042 S. Kedvale	Max	2000s	n.f.	E117	4900 W. Chicago	Captain	2000s	90
E100	6843 S. Harper	Barron	1970s	125	E120	11035 S. Homewood	Charlie Brown	1970s	n.f.
E100	6843 S. Harper	Brown Dog	1990s	124–125	E121	1700 W. 95th	Name Unknown	1970s	n.f.
E101	2240 W. 69th	Mitzi	1970s	n.f.	E122	6858 S. Indiana	Duke	1940s	104

Co.	Address	Firedog	Timeframe	Pages
E122	6858 S. Indiana	Spike	1950s	104–105
E122	6858 S. Indiana	Pepper	1950s	104–105
E122	101 E. 79th	Troubles	1970s	105
E123	5218 S. Western	Moon	1950s	n.f.
E124	4426 N. Kedzie	Whiskers	1970s	47
E124	4426 N. Kedzie	Sparky	1970s	46–47
E124	4426 N. Kedzie	Smokey	1980s	n.f.
E124	4426 N. Kedzie	Barney	1980s	47–48
E124	4426 N. Kedzie	Striker	2000s	48–49
E125	2323 N. Natchez	Queenie	1930s	6
E125	2323 N. Natchez	Chipper	1950s	8, 32
E126	7313 S. Kingston	Snoopy	1970s	105–107
E126	7313 S. Kingston	Rosie	1970s	105–107
E126	7313 S. Kingston	Stuka	1980s	107
E126	7313 S. Kingston	Smokey	2000s	107
E129	8120 S. Ashland	Rosie	1970s	n.f.
E129	8120 S. Ashland	Heidi	1970s	n.f.
CFA	720 W. Vernon Park	Name Unknown	1930s	n.f.
CFA	1310 S. Clinton	Hilly Beans	2000s	91–92
RP	31st & Sacramento	Nellie	1950s	135
RP	31st & Sacramento	Butch	1950s	135
ASR	6400 S. Coast Guard	Lady	1970s	136–137
ASR	Meigs Field	Beau	1980s	136
ASR	Meigs Field	Star	1980s	136

Index by Firedog Name

☙ Index by Firedog Name ☙

Firedog	Co.	Address	Timeframe	Pages	Firedog	Co.	Address	Timeframe	Pages
Snoopy	E82	817 E. 91st	1970s	n.f.	Whiskers	E124	4426 N. Kedzie	1970s	47
Snoopy	E126	7313 S. Kingston	1970s	105–107	Whiskey	E68	1642 N. Kostner	1970s	94–95
Snorkel	E14	1129 W. Chicago	1970s	78	Whitey	E14	509 W. Chicago	1950s	79
Spanner	E19	3423 S. Calumet	1990s	108	Willie	E1	419 S. Wells	1970s	92–93
Sparky	HL21	1501 W. School	1950s	n.f.	Wino	E83	1200 W. Wilson	1980s	9, 28, 59–61
Sparky	E26	10 N. Leavitt	Unknown	n.f.	Wino, Jr.	E83	1200 W. Wilson	1990s	61, 62–63
Sparky	E39	1618 W. 33rd	1960s	130, 132	Wolfie	E97	13359 S. Burley	2000s	n.f.
Sparky	E124	4426 N. Kedzie	1970s	46–47	Yick	E2	2421 S. Lowe	1950s	108–109
Spike	E78	1052 W. Waveland	1960s	35–36	Zimm	SS1	1044 N. Orleans	1970s	43–44
Spike	E122	6858 S. Indiana	1950s	104–105	Zulu	E95	4005 W. West End	1980s	80
Stanley	E47	432 E. Marquette	1970s	118	Unknown	E1	220 S. Franklin	1870s	n.f.
Star	ASR	Meigs Field	1980s	136	Unknown	E1	220 S. Franklin	1870s	n.f.
Stormy	E76	1747 N. Pulaski	1970s	57–58	Unknown	E63	6330 S. Maryland	1890s	n.f.
Stormy II	E76	1747 N. Pulaski	1980s	58–59	Unknown	E19	3444 S. Rhodes	1900s	n.f.
Striker	E124	4426 N. Kedzie	2000s	48–49	Unknown	E40	119 N. Franklin	1900s	n.f.
Stuka	E126	7313 S. Kingston	1980s	107	Unknown	E5	324 S. Desplaines	1910s	n.f.
Susie	E63	6330 S. Maryland	1960s	122–123	Unknown	HL21	1529 N. Belmont	1910s	n.f.
Susie II	E63	6330 S. Maryland	1960s	122	Unknown	E57	2412 W. Haddon	1910s	n.f.
Susie	E95	4005 W. West End	1980s	80	Unknown	E58	95th Street Bridge	1910s	n.f.
Sydney	E95	4005 W. West End	1980s	79	Unknown	S3	5349 S. Wabash	1920s	n.f.
Sydney	E96	439 N. Waller	2000s	96–97	Unknown	E75	6240 S. Peoria	1920s	n.f.
Teddy	E77	1224 S. Komensky	1970s	n.f.	Unknown	HL10	1613 N. Hudson	1920s	n.f.
Teesha	E115	11940 S. Peoria	2000s	102–103	Unknown	E16	23 W. 31st	1920s	n.f.
Thirty	E30	1125 N. Ashland	2000s	36–38	Unknown	E42	55 W. Illinois	1920s	n.f.
Tiger	E114	3542 W. Fullerton	1970s	87	Unknown	E43	2179 N. Stave	1930s	n.f.
Tim O'Reilly	E104	1401 S. Michigan	1950s	103–104	Unknown	E45	4600 S. Cottage Grove	1930s	n.f.
Tinkerbell	E47	423 E. Marquette	2000s	118	Unknown	E89	4456 N. Knox	1930s	n.f.
Tinkerbell	E51	6345 S. Wentworth	1950s	n.f.	Unknown	CFA	720 W. Vernon Park	1930s	n.f.
Tinkerbell II	E47	432 E. Marquette	1960s	n.f.	Unknown	E2	2421 S. Lowe	1940s	n.f.
Tommy	E5	324 S. Desplaines	1950s	90–91	Unknown	S3	5349 S. Wabash	1940s	n.f.
Tonto	E73	8630 S. Emerald	1980s	137	Unknown	E89	3945 W. Peterson	1940s	n.f.
Toughie	S2	114 N. Aberdeen	1950s	129	Unknown	E38	2111 S. Hamlin	1950s	n.f.
Tower	E4	548 W. Division	1980s	40	Unknown	E77	1224 S. Komensky	1950s	n.f.
Trigger	E25	1975 S. Canalport	1950s	n.f.	Unknown	E12	1641 W. Lake	1960s	n.f.
Troubles	E122	101 E. 79th	1970s	105	Unknown	E111	1701 N. Washtenaw	1960s	n.f.

Firedog	Co.	Address	Timeframe	Pages
Unknown	E11	10 E. Hubbard	1970s	n.f.
Unknown	E24	2447 W. Warren	1970s	n.f.
Unknown	E43	2179 N. Stave	1970s	n.f.
Unknown	E44	412 N. Kedzie	1970s	n.f.
Unknown	E54	7101 S. Parnell	1970s	n.f.
Unknown	E121	1700 W. 95th	1970s	n.f.
Unknown	E107	1101 S. California	1980s	n.f.
Unknown	E113	5212 W. Harrison	1980s	n.f.
Unknown	E64	7659 S. Pulaski	1990s	n.f.
Unknown	E107	1101 S. California	1990s	n.f.
Unknown	E115	11940 S. Peoria	1990s	n.f.

Acknowledgments

⚜ Acknowledgments ⚜

Without the generosity and willingness of so many Chicago firefighters to tell us stories, sometimes more than once, this book would not be possible. First and foremost, thank you to the men and women who serve the City of Chicago, the Chicago Fire Department, and the Commissioner's Office. Hopefully this book will appropriately pay tribute to their continual service and dedication to the City of Chicago.

We could not have written this book without the assistance of two incredible people. Heartfelt thanks goes to Gail Orsinger for all her hard work, perpetual encouragement, and objective arbitration when we needed it most. She balanced the job of consultant and "Mom" with unusual grace. Tremendous gratitude also goes to Kate Orsinger for not only creating the "official" logo of the book but for her exceptional patience and enthusiasm throughout the process. As Drew's wife, countless critical nights were lost to firedog research, writing, and conference calls from Washington, D.C., to Chicago.

Significant thanks goes to Chicago Firefighter John Pawelko, who introduced us to our first firehouse dog, Sadie, and initially inspired us to forge ahead, then to Michael Closen, who first urged us to put this idea on paper. We are uniquely indebted to Mike Devine and Chris Hayter for their editorial contributions. To Megan Ryan, we are grateful for your zest in this project, your ability to listen to a story, and your willingness to help whenever we needed it. Chris Demato was there from the beginning with research assistance, constant encouragement, and original ideas. Our Web site would not have been possible without the help of Jeffrey Manning. We are also extremely appreciative of Claude Walker's advice and ideas.

We are grateful for the unconditional support and encouragement of the McGuire Clan: Tony, Lynn, Chris, Megan, Hillary, Eric, Susan, and Jack.

We thank those who gave us an abundance of photographs, and to our photographers, specifically Tim and Sherrie Vermande who spent three days traveling the city to shoot over 20 firedogs. Special thanks go to Chris Cox and his assistant Ed Karpiel for the cover shot. Terry Sullivan was among the first to be enlisted and we truly appreciate the joy he took in accompanying us to the firehouses. Lee Kowalski's generous artwork added a remarkable flavor and charm to this book. Mark Mitchell, Marvin Dembinsky, Jr., James Regan, and the Chicago Fire Department Photo Lab also provided us with invaluable advice and assistance.

We are also indebted to the historians and "fire buffs" who gave us a unique insight into the Chicago Fire Department. Thanks again to Reverend John McNalis, Ken Little, and the Chicago Fire Museum for their unlimited assistance and historical consulting. Batavia, Illinois, Mayor Jeffery D. Schielke not only provided us access to his personal archives, but also allowed us to review the Frank Wiswell Fire Collection (former chief of Midlothian Fire Department), the Bob Freeman Fire Collection (Chicago Fire Department), and the Fred C. "Bud" Richter Fire Collection (former chief of Batavia Fire Department). Many of the photographs and stories in the book are traced back to one of these original collections. Darlene Fillis was one of those rare gems who provided us first hand source material on legendary firedog Felix. She helped keep an unforgettable story alive. Special appreciation goes to Hal Bruno who reviewed the final product and provided a guiding hand when we seemed lost. Without his work in the 1950s, our book would not be as complete as it is today.

Distinguished thanks goes to the administrative staff of the Chicago Fire Department, including Michael Cosgrove and Molly Sullivan. Thanks to the ever-faithful Marge Callahan who worked her magic numerous times for us. We are also indebted to the North Side Irish Fire Brigade and the Gaelic Fire Brigade on the South Side. Thanks also to Karen Kruse, Heather and Matt O'Brien, Martha Powers, CDR Chris Carter, Lt. Brad Kieserman, Flora Clamor, Lydia Plonder, Charlotte Carone, the Ryan family, the Blevins family, the Harts, Kathy Silva, Kathleen Collins, Brian Doherty, Greg Greenwood, Rita Gavin, Connie Jellison, The Cook County Public Defender's Office, the Ferraros, the Dopheides, Cathy Johnson, Ed Karas, Peggy McNamara, Danny Fleis Chacker, Rebecca Morgan, Rose Russell, Linda Niles, Scott Spaw, Chuck Shotwell, Doreen Levy, Margie Mei, Matthew Witt, The DiRusso family, The Chicago Cubs, The Adler Planetarium, and Mary Werderitch.

Lastly, thanks to the quintessential Chicagoan, Rick Orsinger. The former street reporter turned public defender not only showed us the beauty of Chicago, but was always willing to chase a fire anywhere in the city. Your spirit carried this book to print and is always in our hearts.

⚱ Register of Firefighters ⚱
Who Aided in Publication

We know we couldn't possibly record the names of every firefighter who helped us, but the following list is an attempt to individually thank those active and retired firefighters who spent so much of their personal time regaling us with firedog tales. In addition to their stories, many of their most cherished pictures were voluntarily provided to the authors. Without their help, *The Firefighter's Best Friend* would not have been possible. Because they frequently change, the ranks and house affilations were intentionally removed:

Jim Abbott, Bradley Aikens, Dan Allen, Kevin Allen, Manny Almodovar, Jim Altman, Patrick Arnold, Robert Arnoldt, Chris Arroyo, Richard Barker, Roy Barry, Dick Bastain, Larry Beagle, Clarence Berger, Sid Blustain, Robert Boelema, William Boyer, Spike Breitfuss, Sean Burke, Billy Burnam, Jack Calderone, Denise Cantrell, Kevin Casey, Tom Casey, Tom Casey, II, Danny Carbol, Ed Carone, Dan Carrey, William Carroll, Willis Christian, Scott Choate, Robert Cimarolli, Jim Clarke, Rick Cloud, Jerry Cloutier, John Colby, Dwayne Collins, Thomas Collins, Tom Connelly, Tom Cook, Mark Corter, Gary Creager, Mitch Crooker, Tom Deacy, Fernando De Avila, Maria De Caussin, Charlie De Jesus, Mike DelGreco, Tom Dempsey, Sean Devine, Kevin Doherty, Marty Doherty, Bob Dombrowski, Greg Domel, Irving Doucet, Richard Drezek, John Duignan, Jr., Jerry Dwyer, Tim Dwyer, Ron Ellingsen, Joe Felicicchia, Courtney Fields, Rob Fisher, Robert Flynn, Danny Fortuna, Pat Gallagher, Eddy Ganta, James Gaughan, Eddie Gavin, Ed Gill, Drew Goldsmith, John Gollogly, Jesse Gonzales, Dave Gorzycki, Joe Graber, Eugene Green, Chris Greve, John Griffin, Ed Groya, Cat Gulick, Roger Hain, Jim Hampe, David Helstrom, Bill Hendricks, Pat Heneghan, John Herling, Brian Herrli, Sam Holloway, Juan Horton, Larry Howard, Bill Humphrey, Anthony Imparato, Daniel Jallen, Jeff Janusch, Captain Jibbs, James Joyce, John Joyce, William Kapolnek, Ed Keating, Pat Kerr, Brian Kinnear, Bob Kitner, Sully Kolmey, Mort Krogstad, Bill Kugelman, Phil Lamm, John Laporta, Kamran Lawrence, Ronald Larrieu, James Lee, Frankie Lehner, Pamela Lesher, Phil Lesher, Pat Leyden, Pat Lindenmeyer, Phil Little, Steve Little, Dave Loper, Tom Loughney, Thomas Lukaszewicz, Tom Luzak, George Lynch, Wally Lynch, Jim Lyons, Larry Mahler, Scott Malito, Gus Malmtia, Dan Mallmann, Daniel Manobianco, Bob Martin, Mike Matuszewski, John McErlean, Tim McInerney, Pat McMahon, James McNally, William McNamara, Dan McNalis, John Metzger, Don Mikesh, Jermaine Miller, Captain Mindek, Milan Mitrovic, Bob Montalbano, Ozzie Moran, Tom Moran, John Moser, Scott Mulcrone, Reverend Tom Mulcrone, Ed Murphy, James Murphy, John Murray, Sherwood Murray, Leon Muscia, Ken Musial, Greg Niles, Martin Nolan, Karl Norals, Claude Norwood, Gregory Novak, Dennis Novotny, Kevin O'Conner,

Tom O'Donnell, Desi O'Neill, Jean O'Ryan, Hilery O'Shaughnessy, Pawel Osuch, Larry Paller, Linda Parsons, Ed Pereyra, Marty Perez, Scott M. Peterson, Frank Plescia, Ed Ponce, Bob Popp, Curtis Powell, Greg Presny, George Rabiela, Pat "Rack" Reardon, Brian Rafferty, Steve Redick, Gary Reitz, Al Rios, Frank Restivo, Mike Reuter, Hector Rivera, Charlie Rivers, Jim Rockwell, David Rodriguez, Rammon Romo, Jack Rossi, Frank Ruscello, Chris Russel, Jack Russell, Jack Salzman, John Scheinpflug, Bob Schmidt, Marilyn Schriner, Bob Schumacher, Wayne Sieck, Charlie Selinka, Chris Serb, Maureen Skorek, Bob Smith, Steven Smith, Larry Sobek, Paul Sobczak, John Solcani, Brian Stack, John Stalzer, John Stenzlyn, Jr., John Stenzlyn, Sr., Brian Strauss, Don Svachula, Rob Tebbens, Barry Temple, Rich Ternes, Tom Tervanis, Mark Thomas, Bob Twardek, Ed Vale, Glenn Vogrich, Tom Walsh, Hans Wanner, Kevin Ward, Donnell Warrick, Jeff Weber, Tom Welch, Joe Whitlock, Mike Winograd, Bob Wood, Dick Yellis, Curtis Zeigler, Rick Zeigler, Roger Zinchuk, Bob Zollner, and Thomas Zubaty.

⚱ Photo Credits ⚱

Foreword
1. Photo courtesy of the Chicago Fire Museum.
2. Photo courtesy of the Chicago Fire Department.

Preface
1. Painting by Lee Kowalski.

Chapter 1: The Chicago Firedog in History
1. Photo courtesy of the Chicago Fire Museum.
2. Photo courtesy of the Frank McMenamin Collection.
3. Photo courtesy of the Frank McMenamin Collection.
4. Photo courtesy of the Chicago Fire Museum.
5. Photo courtesy of the Chicago Fire Museum.
6. Photo courtesy of the Chicago Fire Museum.
7. Photo by Tim Vermande.
8. Painting by Lee Kowalski.

Chapter 2: The Life of the Chicago Firedog
1. Photo courtesy of the Chicago Fire Museum.
2. Photo courtesy of the Chicago Fire Museum.
3. Photo courtesy of Rob Tebbens.
4. Logo courtesy of Steve Redick.
5. Photo courtesy of the Chicago Fire Museum.

Chapter 3: Legends of the City
Felix
1. Photo courtesy of Darlene Filis.
2. Photo courtesy of the Chicago Fire Museum.
3. Photo courtesy of Darlene Filis.
4. Photo courtesy of the Chicago Fire Museum.
5. Photo courtesy of Darlene Filis.
6. Photo by Trevor J. Orsinger.
7. Photo courtesy of Darlene Filis.
8. Photo by Trevor J. Orsinger.
9. Photo by Trevor J. Orsinger.

Bozo
10. Photo courtesy of Karen Kruse.

Caesar
11. Photo courtesy of the Jeffrey D. Schielke Collection.
12. Photo courtesy of the Jeffrey D. Schielke Collection.
13. Photo by Trevor J. Orsinger.

Chapter 4: North Side Firedogs
Engine 78
1. Photo by Trevor J. Orsinger.
2. Photo by Terry Sullivan.
3. Photo courtesy of the Jeffrey D. Schielke Collection.
4. Photo courtesy of Steve Little.

Engine 30
5. Photo by Terry Sullivan.
6. Photo by Doreen Levy.
7. Photo by Terry Sullivan.
8. Photo courtesy of Milan Mitrovic and the 1988 Chicago Firefighter's Union — Local 2 Yearbook.

Engine 4
9. Photo courtesy of the Jeffrey D. Schielke Collection.
10. Photo courtesy of the Jeffrey D. Schielke Collection.

Engine 20
11. Photo courtesy of the Jeffrey D. Schielke Collection.
12. Photo courtesy of Milan Mitrovic and the 1988 Chicago Firefighter's Union — Local 2 Yearbook.

Snorkel Squad 1
13. Photo courtesy of the Chicago Fire Museum.
14. Photo courtesy of the Chicago Fire Museum.
15. Photo courtesy of the Chicago Fire Museum.
16. Photo courtesy of the Chicago Fire Museum.

Engine 11
17. Photo courtesy of the Chicago Fire Museum.

Engine 124
18. Photo courtesy of James Lee.
19. Photo courtesy of Milan Mitrovic and the 1988 Chicago Firefighter's Union — Local 2 Yearbook.
20. Photo by Terry Sullivan.

Engine 13
21. Photo courtesy of Maureen Skorek.
22. Photo courtesy of Maureen Skorek.
23. Photo courtesy of the Jeffrey D. Schielke Collection.

Hook and Ladder 3
24. Photo courtesy of Clarence Berger.
25. Photo courtesy of Clarence Berger.

Engine 42
26. Photo courtesy of authors' collection.
27. Photo courtesy of the Chicago Fire Museum.
28. Photo courtesy of Tom Casey.

Engine 55
29. Photo courtesy of Sid Blustain.

Engine 56
30. Photo courtesy of the Jeffrey D. Schielke Collection.
31. Photo courtesy of Chicago Fire Department, Engine 56.

32. Photo courtesy of Milan Mitrovic and the 1988 Chicago Firefighter's Union — Local 2 Yearbook.

Engine 76
33. Photo by Drew F. Orsinger.
34. Photo courtesy of Chicago Fire Department, Engine 76.
35. Photo courtesy of Chicago Fire Department, Engine 76.

Engine 83
36. Photo courtesy of the Jeffrey D. Schielke Collection.
37. Photo by Trevor J. Orsinger.

Chapter 5: West Side Firedogs
Engine 18
1. Photo by Tim Vermande.

Engine 67
2. Photo courtesy of the 1976 Chicago Firefighter's Union — Local 2 Yearbook.

Engine 103
3. Photo courtesy of Chicago Fire Department, Engine 103.
4. Photo courtesy of Milan Mitrovic and the 1988 Chicago Firefighter's Union — Local 2 Yearbook.
5. Photo by Tim Vermande.
6. Photo courtesy of Connie Jellison.
7. Photo by Tim Vermande.
8. Photo courtesy of Connie Jellison.

Engine 77
9. Photo courtesy of the Jeffrey D. Schielke Collection.

Engine 66
10. Photo courtesy of the Jeffrey D. Schielke Collection.

Engine 26
11. Photo courtesy of Milan Mitrovic and the 1988 Chicago Firefighter's Union — Local 2 Yearbook.
12. Photo by Drew F. Orsinger.

Engine 14
13. Photo by Tim Vermande.

Engine 95
14. Photo courtesy of Leon Muscia.
15. Photo courtesy of Leon Muscia.

Engine 7
16.Photo courtesy of Milan Mitrovic and the 1988 Chicago Firefighter's Union — Local 2 Yearbook.
17.Photo by Trevor J. Orsinger.

Engine 24
18.Photo courtesy of the Chicago Fire Museum.
19.Photo courtesy of Rob Tebbens.
20.Photo courtesy of the 1976 Chicago Firefighter's Union — Local 2 Yearbook.

Engine 44
21.Photo courtesy of Tom Zubaty.
22.Photo courtesy of Tom Zubaty.
23.Photo courtesy of the Chicago Fire Museum.

Engine 114
24.Photo courtesy of the Chicago Fire Museum.

Engine 85
25.Photo courtesy of Sid Blustain.

Engine 113
26.Photo by Tim Vermande.

Engine 117
27.Photo courtesy of Milan Mitrovic and the 1988 Chicago Firefighter's Union — Local 2 Yearbook.
28.Photo by Tim Vermande.
29.Photo by Tim Vermande.

Engine 5
30.Photo courtesy of the Chicago Fire Museum.
31.Photo courtesy of the Jeffrey D. Schielke Collection.

Chicago Fire Academy
32.Photo courtesy of the Chicago Fire Museum.

Engine 57
33.Photo courtesy of Bob Smith.
34.Photo courtesy of Bud Bertog.

Engine 68
35.Photo courtesy of the 1976 Chicago Firefighter's Union — Local 2 Yearbook.

Engine 96
36.Logo courtesy of Chicago Fire Department, Engine 96.
37.Photo by Tim Vermande.
38.Photo courtesy of Milan Mitrovic and the 1988 Chicago Firefighter's Union — Local 2 Yearbook.
39.Photo courtesy of Bill McNamara.

Chapter 6: South Side Firedogs
Engine 115
1.Photo by Tim Vermande.

2.Photo courtesy of Milan Mitrovic and the 1988 Chicago Firefighter's Union — Local 2 Yearbook.

Engine 104
3.Photo courtesy of Rob Tebbens.

Engine 122
4.Photo courtesy of the Chicago Fire Museum.
5.Photo courtesy of the 1976 Chicago Firefighter's Union — Local 2 Yearbook.

Engine 126
6.Photo by Drew F. Orsinger.
7.Photo courtesy of Milan Mitrovic and the 1988 Chicago Firefighter's Union — Local 2 Yearbook.
8.Photo by Trevor J. Orsinger.

Engine 2
9.Photo courtesy of the Chicago Fire Museum.

Engine 52
10.Photo courtesy of the Jeffrey D. Schielke Collection.

Engine 61
11.Photo by Tim Vermande.
12.Photo by Tim Vermande.

Engine 62
13.Photo by Tim Vermande.
14.Photo by Drew F. Orsinger.

Engine 84
15.Photo courtesy of the Chicago Fire Museum.
16.Photo by Tim Vermande.
17.Photo by Tim Vermande.
18.Photo by Drew F. Orsinger.
19.Photo courtesy of the Chicago Fire Department, Engine 84/Truck 51.

Engine 101
20.Photo by Drew F. Orsinger.
21.Photo courtesy of Milan Mitrovic and the 1988 Chicago Firefighter's Union — Local 2 Yearbook.

Engine 47
22.Photo courtesy of Bob Kitner.

Engine 60
23.Photo by Tim Vermande.
24.Photo courtesy of Sherwood Murray.

Engine 63
25.Photo by Drew F. Orsinger.
26.Photo courtesy of Lee Kowalski.
27.Photo courtesy of the Jeffrey D. Schielke Collection.

Engine 80
28.Photo courtesy of the Jeffrey D. Schielke Collection.
29.Photo courtesy of Milan Mitrovic and the 1988 Chicago Firefighter's Union — Local 2 Yearbook.

Engine 100
30.Photo courtesy of Milan Mitrovic and the 1988 Chicago Firefighter's Union — Local 2 Yearbook.

Engine 28
31.Photo by Trevor J. Orsinger.
32.Photo courtesy of Sherwood Murray.

Engine 29
33.Photo by Jim Regan.
34.Photo by Trevor J. Orsinger.

Engine 34
35.Photo courtesy of the Chicago Fire Museum.

Engine 39
36.Photo courtesy of the Chicago Fire Museum.

Engine 41
37.Photo courtesy of the Chicago Fire Museum.

Engine 50
38.Photo courtesy of Jack Russell.
39.Photo by Tim Vermande.
40.Photo by Tim Vermande.
41.Photo by Tim Vermande.

Air and Sea Rescue
42.Photo courtesy of Milan Mitrovic and the 1988 Chicago Firefighter's Union — Local 2 Yearbook.
43. Photo courtesy of Milan Mitrovic and the 1988 Chicago Firefighter's Union — Local 2 Yearbook.
44. Photo courtesy of the Chicago Fire Museum.

Engine 74
45.Photo courtesy of the Jeffrey D. Schielke Collection.

Engine 73
46.Photo courtesy of Milan Mitrovic and the 1988 Chicago Firefighter's Union — Local 2 Yearbook.

Engine 45
47.Photo courtesy of Jim McNally.
48.Photo courtesy of Jim McNally.
49.Photo courtesy of the Chicago Fire Museum.

Lake Claremont Press is . . .

Great Chicago Fires: Historic Blazes That Shaped a City
by David Cowan
Perhaps no other city in America identifies itself with fire quite like Chicago does; certainly no other city cites a great conflagration as the cornerstone of its will and identity. Yet the Great Chicago Fire was not the only infamous blaze the city would see. Acclaimed author and veteran firefighter David Cowan tells the story of the other "great" Chicago fires, noting the causes, consequences, and historical context of each—from the burning of Fort Dearborn in 1812 to the Iroquois Theater disaster to the Our Lady of the Angels school fire and many more.
1-893121-07-0, 2001, paperback, 167 pages, 86 photos, $19.95

Chicago's Midway Airport: The First Seventy-Five Years
by Christopher Lynch
Midway was Chicago's first official airport, and for decades it was the busiest airport in the nation, and then the world. Its story is an American story, encompassing heroes and villains, generosity and greed, boom and bust, progress and decline, and in the final chapter, rebirth. Join Christopher Lynch as he combines oral histories, narrative, and historic and contemporary photos to celebrate the rich and exciting 75-year history of this colorful airport and the evolution of aviation right along with it.
1-893121-18-6, 2003, paperback, 201 pages, 205 photos, $19.95

Near West Side Stories: Struggles for Community in Chicago's Maxwell Street Neighborhood
by Carolyn Eastwood
Near West Side Stories is an ongoing story of unequal power in Chicago. Four representatives of immigrant and migrant groups that have had a distinct territorial presence in the area—one Jewish, one Italian, one African-American, and one Mexican—reminisce fondly on life in the old neighborhood and tell of their struggles to save it and the 120-year-old Maxwell Street Market that was at its core. *Near West Side Stories* brings this saga of community strife up to date, while giving a voice to the everyday people who were routinely discounted or ignored in the big decisions that affected their world.
Winner of the *Midwest Independent Publishers Association (MIPA) Book Award (2nd Place in the Regional category)*, 2002.
1-893121-09-7, 2002, paperback, 355 pages, 113 photos, $17.95

The Chicago River: A Natural and Unnatural History
by Libby Hill
When French explorers Jolliet and Marquette used the Chicago portage to access the Mississippi River system, the Chicago River was but a humble, even sluggish, stream in the right place at the right time. That's the story of the making of Chicago. This is the other story—the story of the making and perpetual re-making of a river by everything from pre-glacial forces to the interventions of an emerging and mighty city. Author Libby Hill brings together years of original research and the contributions of dozens of experts to tell the Chicago River's epic tale from its conception in prehistoric bedrock to the glorious rejuvenation it's undergoing today, and every exciting episode in between.
Winner of the *American Regional History Publishing Award (1st Place for the Midwest Region)*, 2001.
Winner of the *Midwest Independent Publisher Association (MIPA) Book Award (2nd Place in the History category)*, 2000.
1-893121-02-X, 2000, paperback, 302 pages, 78 photos, $16.95

The Hoofs and Guns of the Storm: Chicago's Civil War Connections

by Arnie Bernstein; Foreword by Senator Paul Simon

While America's Civil War was fought on Confederate battlefields, Chicago played a crucial role in the Union's struggle toward victory. *The Hoofs and Guns of the Storm* takes you through a whirlwind of 19th century events that created the foundation for modern-day Chicago. Discover the role Chicago played in Abraham Lincoln's unlikely bid for the Presidency, Mary Todd Lincoln's trials and tribulations after her husband's assassination, how Chicago's Union Blue was streaked with hints of Confederate Gray, and much more!

1-893121-06-2, September 2003, paperback, approx. 280 pages, $15.95

Hollywood on Lake Michigan: 100 Years of Chicago and the Movies

by Arnie Bernstein

From the earliest film studios, when one out of every five movies was made in Chicago, to today's thriving independent film scene, the Windy City has been at the forefront of American moviemaking. Join writer/film historian Arnie Bernstein as he honors Chicago and Chicagoans for their active role in a century of filmmaking. Exclusive interviews with current directors, actors, writers, and other film professionals; visits to movie locations and historical sites; and fascinating tales from the silent era are all a part of this spirited and definitive look at our "Hollywood on Lake Michigan."

Winner of the *American Regional History Publishing Award (1st Place for the Midwest Region)*, 2000.

0-9642426-2-1, 1998, paperback, 364 pages, 80 photos, $15.00

GHOSTS AND GRAVEYARDS

NEW!

Creepy Chicago: A Ghosthunter's Tales of the City's Scariest Sites

by Ursula Bielski

For readers ages 8-12. You are about to take an armchair excursion through one of America's greatest cities! Like millions of tourists who visit "The Windy City" each year, you'll make stops at world-famous museums, marvel at towering skyscrapers, explore the town's terrific neighborhoods, and speed along the shore of Lake Michigan on fabulous Lake Shore Drive. But unlike those other tourists, we won't be searching for priceless paintings, pioneering architecture, local heritage, or luscious views. We're on the lookout for . . . g-g-g-g-ghosts!

1-893121-15-1, August 2003, paperback, 136 pages, $8.00

Chicago Haunts: Ghostlore of the Windy City

by Ursula Bielski

From ruthless gangsters to restless mail order kings, from the Fort Dearborn Massacre to the St. Valentine's Day Massacre, the phantom remains of the passionate people and volatile events of Chicago history have made the Second City second to none in the annals of American ghostlore. Bielski captures over 160 years of this haunted history with her unique blend of lively storytelling, in-depth historical research, exclusive interviews, and insights from parapsychology. Called "a masterpiece of the genre," "a must read," and "an absolutely first-rate book" by reviewers, *Chicago Haunts* continues to earn the praise of critics and readers alike.

0-9642423-7-2. 1998, paperback, 277 pages, 29 photos, $15.00

More Chicago Haunts: Scenes from Myth and Memory
by Ursula Bielski
Chicago. A town with a past. A people haunted by its history in more ways than one. A "windy city" with tales to tell...Bielski is back with more history, more legends, and more hauntings, including the personal scary stories of *Chicago Haunts* readers. Read about the Ovaltine factory haunts, the Monster of 63rd Street's castle of terror, phantom blueberry muffins, Wrigley Field ghosts, Al Capone's yacht, and 45 other glimpses into the haunted myths and memories of Chicagoland.
1-893121-04-6, 2000, paperback, 312 pages, 50 photos, $15.00

Graveyards of Chicago: The People, History, Art, and Lore of Cook County Cemeteries
by Matt Hucke and Ursula Bielski
Discover a Chicago that exists just beneath the surface—about six feet under! Ever wonder where Al Capone is buried? How about Clarence Darrow? Muddy Waters? Harry Caray? Or maybe Brady Bunch patriarch Robert Reed? And what really lies beneath home plate at Wrigley Field? Graveyards of Chicago answers these and other cryptic questions as it charts the lore and lure of Chicago's ubiquitous burial grounds. Grab a shovel and tag along as Ursula Bielski, local historian and author of *Chicago Haunts*, and Matt Hucke, photographer and creator of www.graveyards.com, unearth the legends and legacies that mark Chicago's silent citizens—from larger-than-lifers and local heroes, to clerics and comedians, machine mayors and machine-gunners.
0-9642426-4-8, 1999, paperback, 228 pages, 168 photos, $15.00

Haunted Michigan: Recent Encounters with Active Spirits
by Rev. Gerald S. Hunter
Within these pages you'll not find ancient ghost stories or legendary accounts of spooky events of long ago. Instead, Rev. Hunter shares his investigations into modern ghost stories—active hauntings that continue to this day. *Haunted Michigan* uncovers a chilling array of local spirits in its tour of the two peninsulas. Wherever you may dwell, these tales of Michigan's ethereal residents are sure to make you think about the possibility, as Hunter suggests, that we are not alone within the confines of our happy homes. So wait until the shadows of night have cast a pall over the serenity of your peaceful abode. Then snuggle into your favorite overstuffed chair, pour yourself a bracing bolt of 80-proof courage, and open your mind to the presence of the paranormal which surrounds us all.
1-893121-29-1, October 2000, paperback, 207 pages, 20 photos, $12.95

More Haunted Michigan: New Encounters with Ghosts of the Great Lakes State
by Rev. Gerald S. Hunter
Rev. Hunter invited readers of *Haunted Michigan* to open their minds to the presence of the paranormal all around them. They opened their minds . . . and unlocked a grand repository of their own personal supernatural experiences. Hunter investigated these modern, active hauntings and recounts the most chilling and most unusual here for you, in further confirmation that the Great Lakes State may be one of the most haunted places in the country. Join Hunter as he tours the state, documenting the unexplainable and exploring the presence of the paranormal in our lives.
1-893121-29-1, February 2003, paperback, 231 pages, 19 photos, $15.00

NEW!

A Native's Guide to Northwest Indiana

by Mark Skertic

At the southern tip of Lake Michigan, in the crook between Chicagoland and southwestern Michigan, lies Northwest Indiana, a region of natural diversity, colorful history, abundant recreational opportunities, small town activities, and urban diversions. Whether you're a life-long resident, new to the area, or just passing through, let native Mark Skertic be your personal tour guide of the best the region has to offer. Full of places, stories, and facts that sometimes even locals don't know about. Skertic's guide will help you create your own memorable excursions into Northwest Indiana.

1-893121-08-9, August 2003, paperback, $15.00

NEW!

A Native's Guide to Chicago, 4th Edition

by Lake Claremont Press; Edited by Sharon Woodhouse

Venture into the nooks and crannies of everyday Chicago with the newest edition of the comprehensive budget guide that started our press. Over 400 pages of free, inexpensive, and unusual things to do in the Windy City make this the perfect resource for tourists, business travelers, visiting suburbanites, and resident Chicagoans.

1-893121-23-2, September 2003, paperback, $15.95

A Cook's Guide to Chicago

by Marilyn Pocius

Pocius shares the culinary expertise she acquired in chef school and through years of footwork around the city searching for the perfect ingredients and supplies. Each section includes store listings, cooking tips, recipes, and "Top 10 ingredients" lists to give readers a jump start on turning their kitchens into dens of worldly cuisine. Includes an easy-to-use index with over 2,000 ingredients! Recommended by the *Chicago Tribune*, *Chicago Sun-Times*, *Chicago Reader*, *Daily Southtown*, *Local Palate*, Pioneer Press newspapers, *Chicago Life*, ChicagoCooks.com, FoodLines.com, ethnic-grocery-tours.com, and more!

1-893121-16-X, 2002, paperback, 278 pages, $15.00

Ticket to Everywhere: The Best of *Detours* Travel Column

by Dave Hoekstra; Foreword by Studs Terkel

Chicago Sun-Times columnist Dave Hoekstra has compiled 66 of his best road trip explorations into the offbeat people, places, events, and history of the greater Midwest and Route 66 areas. Whether covering the hair museum in Independence, Missouri; Wisconsin's "Magical Mustard Tour"; the Ohio Tiki bar on the National Register of Historic Places; Detroit's polka-dot house; or Bloomington, Illinois—home to beer nuts, Hoekstra's writings will delight readers and instruct tourists. A literary favorite of daytrippers, adventurers, and armchair travelers alike!

1-893121-11-9, 2000, paperback, 227 pages, 70 photos, 9 maps, $15.95

ORDER FORM

Title	Qty.	Total
The Firefighter's Best Friend	_____ @ $19.95 =	_____
Great Chicago Fires	_____ @ $19.95 =	_____
Chicago's Midway Airport	_____ @ $19.95 =	_____
Near West Side Stories	_____ @ $17.95 =	_____
The Chicago River	_____ @ $16.95 =	_____
The Hoofs and Guns of the Storm	_____ @ $15.95 =	_____
Hollywood on Lake Michigan	_____ @ $15.00 =	_____
Creepy Chicago	_____ @ $ 8.00 =	_____
Chicago Haunts	_____ @ $15.00 =	_____
More Chicago Haunts	_____ @ $15.00 =	_____
Graveyards of Chicago	_____ @ $15.00 =	_____
A Native's Guide to NW Indiana	_____ @ $15.00 =	_____
A Native's Guide to Chicago, 4th Ed.	_____ @ $15.95 =	_____
A Cook's Guide to Chicago	_____ @ $15.00 =	_____
Ticket to Everywhere	_____ @ $15.95 =	_____
_____	_____ @ $____ =	_____
_____	_____ @ $____ =	_____

Subtotal: _____

Less Discount: _____

New Subtotal: _____

8.75% sales tax for Illinois Residents: _____

Shipping: _____

TOTAL: _____

4650 N. Rockwell St.
Chicago, IL 60625
(773) 583-7800 phone
(773) 583-7877 fax
lcp@lakeclaremont.com
www.lakeclaremont.com

PURCHASE MULTIPLE TITLES AND SAVE!

2 books	–	10% discount
3–4 books	–	20% discount
5–9 books	–	25% discount
10+ books	–	40% discount

LOW SHIPPING FEES

- $2.50 for the first book
- $.50 for each additional book
- Maximum charge: $8.00

ORDER BY MAIL, PHONE, FAX, OR E-MAIL

All of our books have a no-hassle,
100% money-back guarantee!

Lake Claremont Press books can be found at Chicagoland bookstores and online at Amazon.com, bn.com, and others.

Name: _____

Address: _____

City: _____ State: _____ Zip: _____

e-mail address: _____

Please enclose check, money order, or credit card information.

Visa/Mastercard # _____ Exp. date: _____

Signature _____

Also from Lake Claremont Press . . .

Great Chicago Fires:
Historic Blazes That Shaped a City
by David Cowan

The Hoofs and Guns of the Storm:
Chicago's Civil War Connections
by Arnie Bernstein

Chicago's Midway Airport:
The First Seventy-Five Years
by Christopher Lynch

Near West Side Stories: Struggles for
Community in Chicago's
Maxwell Street Neighborhood
by Carolyn Eastwood

The Chicago River:
A Natural and Unnatural History
by Libby Hill

Hollywood on Lake Michigan:
100 Years of Chicago and the Movies
by Arnie Bernstein

"The Movies Are": Carl Sandburg's Film
Reviews and Essays, 1920–1928
Edited by Arnie Bernstein
Introduction by Roger Ebert

Literary Chicago: A Book Lover's
Tour of the Windy City
by Greg Holden

Graveyards of Chicago:
The People, History, Art, and Lore
of Cook County Cemeteries
by Matt Hucke and Ursula Bielski

Chicago Haunts: Ghostlore
of the Windy City
by Ursula Bielski

More Chicago Haunts: Scenes
from Myth and Memory
by Ursula Bielski

Creepy Chicago: A Ghosthunter's Tales of the
City's Scariest Sites
by Ursula Bielski

Haunted Michigan: Recent
Encounters with Active Spirits
by Rev. Gerald S. Hunter

More Haunted Michigan: New Encounters with
Ghosts of the Great Lakes State
by Rev. Gerald S. Hunter

Muldoon: A True Chicago Ghost Story:
Tales of a Forgotten Rectory
by Rocco A. Facchini and
Daniel J. Facchini

A Cook's Guide to Chicago
by Marilyn Pocius

A Native's Guide to Chicago, 4th Edition
by Lake Claremont Press
Edited by Sharon Woodhouse

A Native's Guide to Northwest Indiana
by Mark Skertic

Ticket to Everywhere:
The Best of Detours *Travel Column*
by Dave Hoekstra

COMING SOON

The Streets & San Man's
Guide to Chicago Eats
by Dennis Foley

The Politics of Place: A History
of Zoning in Chicago
by Joseph Schwieterman and
Dana Caspall

The Golden Age of Chicago
Children's Television
by Ted Okuda and Jack Mulqueen

Finding Your Chicago Ancestors
by Grace DuMelle

♨ About the Authors ♨

A graduate of the John Marshall Law School in Chicago, Trevor Orsinger earned a B.Ph. in philosophy from the Catholic University of America in Washington, D.C. He has published over fifteen articles, co-authored two law review articles, and written several newspaper columns.

Lieutenant Drew Orsinger earned a B.S. in government from the United States Coast Guard Academy in 1996 and is currently a United States Coast Guard Officer in Washington, D.C. Drew has published numerous papers for various government agencies on maritime migration. Both Trevor and Drew grew up in the Chicago area and attended high school at St. Ignatius College Preparatory, across the street from Engine 18 on Roosevelt Road in Chicago.

Prior to the publication of *The Firefighter's Best Friend*, the book was featured in the popular *Dogs with Jobs* television series on the National Geographic Channel, because of its special segment on cover dog *Thirty* from Chicago's Engine 30 on Division Street. For more information on this show and Chicago firedogs and firedog history, visit the Orsinger's website at www.firehousedogs.com.